DATE DUE

NO 10 '98		

DEMCO 38-296

PERFORMANCE POWER

Winning Ways to Face Your Audience

Gloria Shafer

Mellen University Press
Lewiston/Queenston/Lampeter

Library of Congress Cataloging-in-Publication Data

Shafer, Gloria.
  Performance Power : winning ways to face your audience / Gloria
Shafer.
      p.   cm.
  Includes bibliographical references.
  ISBN 0-7734-9924-5
  1. Stage fright. 2. Performance--Psychological aspects.
I. Title.
BF575.F2S47   1992
158' .2--dc20   92-2611
                                                                      CIP

Editorial Inquiries and Order Fulfillment:

The Edwin Mellen Press
Box 450
Lewiston, New York
USA 14092

Printed in the United States of America

To my family and all those
who inspired this book

Table of Contents

Table of Contents

Performance Power: Winning Ways to Face Your Audience

Enjoy appearing in public and taking center stage.
This book tells how to overcome stage fright and make
you successful and secure before an audience.

Think of friends, relatives or celebrities who seem
completely at ease in front of groups or on stage. Do
they know something you don't know? In this book
I will cover the latest scientific evidence sprinkled
with age-old secrets on how to gain performance power.
Everything you always wanted to know about overcoming
stage fright is in this step-by-step guide which will
lead you to the magical land where fear is harnessed
and butterflies fly in formation.

Foreword by Kenneth Greenspan, M.D.

Performing on the various stages of life, many of us experience a transcendental phenomenon called "the adrenalin high," or "peak performance," while others experience tension and panic. It has been scientifically demonstrated that injecting adrenalin into non-anxious and happy individuals produces excitement, whereas it produces increased tension and panic in people who are initially anxious. These findings suggest that our state of being at the moment of performance (adrenalin injection) may determine whether we experience a peak performance, or stage fright. Dr. Shafer provides us with various psycho-physiological techniques and cognitive and spiritual insights for enhancing our state of being. The ultimate conquest of performance anxiety lies not just in the practice of these techniques, but in their integration into our lifestyles and attitudes.

Stage fright, or performance anxiety, is an encapsulation of our many fears of living in a single moment of truth. It is the result of our fear of expressing who we are to the many mini-audiences we encounter on a daily basis. It can be viewed as a spot-lighted duel between our innate desire to express ourselves and our fear of exposure. Stage fright is a distress response, and its ultimate transformation into peak performance is aided by the technologies and insights of stress management.

One dynamic of stress management is the "fight-flight" response initially described in the 1930s by Dr. Cannon at Harvard. He described the physiological response that occurred in animals whose immediate survival was at risk. This same response has persisted through evolution and occurs in humans who are called upon to perform. The fight-flight response, like stress, is neither good nor bad. Indeed, an optimal level is consistent with peak performance. Like a violin string, optimal tautness produces an optimal note; too little or too much produces dystonia. For many of us, the fight-flight response is prolonged and produces a state of imbalance and distress. The techniques discussed by Dr. Shafer are designed to regain control of the psychophysiological, cognitive and spiritual imbalance that results.

Cannon's animal sensing physical danger becomes hyperalert and quickly surveys the environment. Any moves in the bushes nearby are interpreted to be allies of the enemy. This allows the animal to survive and, indeed, is useful when humans confront physical danger. It is not helpful in a performance situation. When we are to perform on stage, however, and are frightened, we automatically become hyperalert and scan the environment for any sound or appearance that indicates disapproval. We shift our focus from our inner center and its connections to others and (in its worse sense) to the enemy called the audience.

As we make this shift, we lose our focused performance. I have had many patients who, while gifted performers, nevertheless agonized and continually scanned the audiences to see who was not responding rather than be aware of the task at hand and focus on those most responsive. During the search for disapproval we are in a continual state of mental distress and spiritual isolation. Our "observing self" (scanning) is not integrated with our "participating self" (performance). This unity is essential if we are to shift from stage fright into a peak performance state. Dr. Shafer is able to give the reader insight into the creative process and describes various centering techniques to enhance our many performances.

In addition to hyperalertness, total body muscles tighten and this prepares the animal's muscles for fight or flight. The human neocortex has the refined ability to selectively tone and relax particular muscle groups as each movement in each performance unfolds. The whole body tension of distress blunts this refined human capacity. In addition, hypertonic facial and vocal cord muscles signal our brain that there is danger and our audience that we are not natural. Dr. Shafer discusses various relaxation and yoga techniques to help control this imbalanced state.

The stress response also produces hypertonic sympathetic nervous system arousal with increased pulse rate, respiratory rate, and adrenalin (amongst many other stress changes). If we are focused and relaxed, these changes will be experienced as pleasurable excitement and will breathe life into our performance. If we are fearful, however, these changes intensify the imbalanced loop of distress and performance anxiety.

Techniques for preventing performance anxiety and enhancing the probability of peak performance fall in three categories: the psychophysiological, the cognitive, and the spiritual. It is recommended that you exercise the psychophysiological first, and when fully relaxed and centered, work with the cognitive and spiritual aspects of the training. Our being is more receptive to new information when we are centered and relaxed. It is best if the affirmations and visualizations focus on the present tense, our connection with others and with the full acceptance of ourselves. "I am what I am."

The moment of truth on the stage is made up of many less magnified moments in which we sit in judgment of others and therefore ourselves. As Dr. Shafer shows us, we now project this self-judgment onto the audience. It is ultimately the attitude of separateness and judgment that produces performance anxiety. (Our lives are comprised of many small stages, and our fear of judgment -- the verdict of the public -- invades not only our expressive self, but our capacity for health and joy.) An attitude of suspending judgment and seeking common bonds with others allows us to continually be united with our many audiences. This is, therefore, a book not only for those wishing to enhance their performance, but for all of us as we self-express and connect with others on the grand stage of life.

Kenneth Greenspan, M.D. is an Assistant Professor of Clinical Psychiatry at the College of Physicians and Surgeons, Columbia University. For many years he served as Director for the Laboratory and Center for Stress Related Disorders at the New York State Psychiatric Institute of Columbia Presbyterian Medical Center.

A major voice in stress management, Dr. Greenspan has been an advisor to the President's Council on Physical Fitness, Health, Education and Welfare, Division on Prevention, the American Red Cross, the United Federation of Teachers, Fire Dispatchers, New York City, Metropolitan Life Insurance Company, and the Surgeon General, United States.

He is the author of over 20 articles and monographs, and has appeared as an eminent authority on stress for nationwide television and print interviews.

Acknowledgments

I owe a great deal of thanks to many people who lent support and encouragement to this project. In particular, I wish to thank Frank Corsaro, head of Actors' Studio, opera and stage director, who shared with me his professional and creative experience; to Kenneth Greenspan, M.D., an eminent authority on stress, who graciously contributed his research studies and clinical findings, as well as providing the preface to this book. Equally valued were the profound insights and discussions with Lawrence Hatterer, M.D., leading psychoanalyst and author of The Creative Artist in Society and Raoul Felder, acclaimed matrimonial attorney, who offered invaluable advise and personal experiences. For candidly answering my queries as to how she conquered her own fears, I am grateful to Barbara Gordon, author of I'm Dancing as Fast as I Can.

I was fortunate enough to have author Gay Talese; actor Eli Wallach; comedian and author Alan King; artistic director and co-founder of the Circle in the Square Theater, Theodore Mann; cinema writer, playwright and author, Leonard Gershe; beauty consultant Georgette Klinger; member of the voice faculty of the Juilliard School of Music and conductor of vocal master classes worldwide, Daniel Ferro; jazz pianist Marian McPartland; jazz dance teacher and lecturer, Luigi; Director of Broadcast Services for CBS, Robert Rush; matrimonial attorney Elaine Shepps; psychiatrist, musician, and athlete, Daniel Kaplowitz, who read and endorsed the manuscript. The secretarial talents of Nancy McGuire, as always, were invaluable. Finally, I extend my gratitude to all those named and unnamed who believed in me.

A Personal Memoir

As performers we all have a beginning -- that first electric moment when we know that we can sing, or act, or play an instrument with a love and a power different from any other feeling.

My beginning came at the age of three as I stood beside my mother at the grocer's, humming and singing with an abandon which is only that of a child. A woman approached my mother: "Miss, is this your daughter? Do you know that she has a beautiful voice?" I saw the look of admiration in the woman's face -- the gleam of pride mixed with astonishment in my mother's eyes. And though I didn't completely understand her words, I instinctively realized, for the first time, that there was something special about my voice, about me. Two years later, my first day in school, the teacher asked us to stand up and give our names. "I am Gloria," I piped up. "I sing."

Ultimately, my parents enrolled me in the Juilliard Preparatory School. I sang publicly through those early years -- once for the Mayor of the City of New York -- and steadily won honors and prizes, all without so much as a hint of stage fright. Then one day in the late 1950's, I found myself, at age fifteen, standing before a microphone on the Paul Whiteman TV Teen Show. Moments before the orchestra began I went completely blank in terror. I couldn't remember a word of "Musetta's Waltz!" I froze. Before I had time to think, however, the sound of the orchestra engulfed me like a great wave and carried me forward, and all self-consciousness, all panic drained away. As if by magic, the words returned as I began to sing.

Yes, stage fright had struck, but I'd escaped its clutches! And more than anything else, this experience, at once so terrifying yet so exhilarating, infused me with the ecstasy of the performer's "high." I was hooked.

Many wonderful appearances followed -- opera, symphonic concerts, musical theatre. Eventually I took a professional hiatus to raise two children and devote myself to domestic life, yet I never ceased practicing and performing locally. Later, I returned to Columbia University and earned a doctorate in Music. I went on to assume several teaching positions.

Then, as chance would have it, a conductor friend and I accidentally met after twenty years, and he invited me to sing a series of arias with his fine orchestra in Florida, a major appearance. I was thrilled, yet at the same time apprehensive. How was I going to make this a positive experience? I could no longer depend on the self-confidence of youth to pull me through! How would I get a handle on my emotions so that the original, accomplished "me" could shine through?

I delved in to all the prevailing techniques, theories and practices -- both conservative and radical -- on stage fright. I scoured libraries, consulted physicians, took private courses from top experts in the field. This book is the summation of all that I learned in preparation for that first Florida performance, which did turn out to be the professional and personal triumph I'd hoped for, and beyond.

But perhaps that sounds too simple, too easy. It was not, of course. Through each technique, through each new practice, I discovered another layer of fear, and of resistance to fear. As a result of my struggles with stage fright, and by talking to others in the field, I concluded that stage fright is not a simple thing. It is, if you will, an accumulation of many, many fears of a lifetime, which manifest themselves at or in anticipation of appearing before an audience. They do so because we believe, rightly or wrongly, that everything we have is on the line and that we will be judged as never before.

These fears exist in roughly this form for anyone who appears before an audience: teachers, salespeople, lawyers, clergy, etc. And I conclude that whoever you are, whatever you do, you will have to face your fears and work through them. It may be a short process or a long one, but there is no escape from it. Nor should you want to escape; this is one of the most important parts of becoming who you are. It may be difficult, but this is where your personal struggle, and adventure, takes place.

After that Florida experience, I found performing in public more enjoyable than ever. I continued to practice the various techniques and self-help remedies, incorporating one or more into my daily routine. My search to make the "butterflies fly in formation" is an ongoing one. Auspiciously, in November of 1989 I was chosen to open the Virginia Slims Championship at Madison Square Garden with our national anthem to thousands of tennis lovers. As I walked to the center of the huge arena eager to make each performance a peak experience, I called upon the techniques and practices I believed in. Each time I sang the "Star- Spangled Banner" it was a great personal triumph.

For me every appearance is a celebration - a special event, a commitment to excellence and personal growth. I happily share my secrets, tools and discoveries with you.

"The human brain is a wonderful thing. It
operates from the moment you're born, until
the first time you get up to make a speech."

(Howard Goshorn, from <u>How to Speak Like a Pro</u>)

PART I

STAGE FRIGHT

CHAPTER 1
STAGE FRIGHT: WHAT IS IT?

I've always been nervous before I appear on stage. The days and hours before are often filled with vague dread, but it's the moments before I actually go on that fear hits the hardest. I doubt my abilities. I doubt the humanity of the audience, but most of all I wonder why I ever chose such a precarious course in my life as to appear regularly before an audience. The fact is, I am scared. In this situation everyone is. If they tell you they are not, well don't believe it. The dictionary definition of stage fright is "nervousness felt at appearing before an audience." To those who have been victim of stage fright, however, those words are wholly inadequate to describe the sensation.

What can entirely describe the shaky hands, sweaty palms, wobbly knees, muscle tremors, queasy stomach, dry throat, fast breathing, memory loss, accelerated heartbeat, excess adrenalin and worse? Certainly not the mere word, "nervousness."

If there is anything at all reassuring about stage fright, it is its universal range. It can afflict performers of all kinds, from the amateur at her first recital to the most illustrious superstar. It is often felt by people addressing a business meeting, by Little League coaches, by job applicants before interviews, by club officers, by members of church groups, and sometimes even in family gatherings. In short, by anyone who appears before an audience.

It is perhaps best recognized in the world of theater and stage, and there its known effects have often been devastating. Helen Hayes, the First Lady of the Broadway stage, regularly went stone deaf before each performance. Singer Carly Simon actually stopped performing for five years because she couldn't bear having to deal with the fear. Even seasoned performers can feel the symptoms building days in advance, and the fear can be overwhelming. Said Alicia de Larrocha, one of America's most accomplished concert pianists, "Sometimes I think, what if there is an earthquake or fire or something? Then I won't have to play."

For good reason, some performers fear the onset of stage fright. Aside from robbing the artist of a fine performance, severe stage fright can actually cause serious deterioration of the voice. It can rob us of strength and creativity, put our feelings out of touch, and cause us to fear the very act -- performing -- which gives our lives joy and meaning.

In reality, stage fright is a symptom, or set of symptoms -- not a cause. It is because performing puts us so much on the line, brings us so close to the core of our being, that it brings up so many fears. A complex of fears: failing to meet audience expectations; of being less than perfect; of overall humiliation; of revealing the real and frightened person underneath. We are rarely so vulnerable as when we stand before an audience, and rarely is the fear so strong. Many people would rather risk bullets than speak before an audience, so powerful are the fears which arise.

At the same time, however, stage fright is neither entirely unmanageable, nor, strangely enough, entirely negative. The same feelings which produce stage fright can, if we begin to explore and work with ourselves, be seen as part of the creative process, as essential to creativity itself. In time, we will be able to fully understand actress Sarah Bernhardt, who was asked by a young ingenue, "What is this stage fright I hear so much about? I've never had it."

Said the great Bernhardt: "It will come -- with talent."

In a way, though, stage fright is not too different from Amarillo Slim's definition of championship poker -- itself a form of performing. Said the seven-time champion, "In the end, boy, it's all a matter of what you think of yourself."

CHAPTER 2

THE AUDIENCE

"And you look out at the audience -- a terrifying
monster with a thousand heads."
                            -Ronald Colman

"There are some things you learn best in calm, and some
in storm. You learn the delivery of a part only before
an audience."
                            -Willa Cather

Why We Perform

     Mae West told her biographer, Charlotte Chandler,
"I heard the applause -- applause just for me -- and I
knew they really liked me. I've never been more secure
than when I'm on stage."

     When she made her debut at Brooklyn's Royal
Theater, the legendary Mae fell hopelessly in love.
"It was my first love affair with my audience and it
lasted all my life." For her, performing was the only
thing that mattered: only then did she feel alive.

     Nor was Mae West alone with these feelings.
Beverly Sills, opera star and director of The New York
City Opera, confesses, "I just couldn't wait to get on
stage, I needed to share the joyfulness that I felt
when I sang. I like to be with people." When on
stage, she felt at home. This element of relaxed

happiness and ease is the mark of many an experienced performer. It is their reward for many years of practice.

Learning to perform successfully -- whether in show business or simply speaking before any group -- is worth the effort. Communicating with an audience is a great high. Sharing through performance is frequently satisfying, and can make our lives more meaningful. For performing is a sharing experience -- meeting with other human beings emotionally and spiritually. We take the focus off ourselves and put it on something larger, and doing so we bring ourselves and the audience together in a shared experience. This is the exciting dynamic involvement. Your goal, then, is to touch and move the audience.

But what is an audience? While, as Shakespeare said, all men and women are merely players on the stage of the world, they are also an audience. The word is derived from the Latin audiere, to hear. Only when we are asleep or quietly alone, not listening to radio or watching TV, are we not acting as an audience. And since to listen is an activity, it is best for the performer to understand that the audience is not simply a passive group just sitting there. It is necessary, then that a performer meet his audience at what actor/author Joseph Chaikin calls the performing level -- facing an audience made up of other actors.

There are, of course, different types of audiences. Captive audiences are familiar to all of us: students in a required course; defendants and jurors in trials; a reluctant congregation at a religious service; managers or union members at compulsory meetings. You're a captive audience if you happen to sit next to a talkative stranger on a crowded plane. For the performer, it sometimes takes a greater effort simply to capture the attention of such an audience than if they were voluntary. Successful teachers, lawyers, and clergymen -- not to mention salespeople -- work hard at creating the enthusiasm and contagious interest necessary to draw in a group of people who initially, at any rate, would rather be someplace else.

That does not mean, though, that a performer before an elective audience necessarily has it any easier. If people have paid for the privilege of listening to you, they expect to be entertained, instructed, or inspired, depending upon whether you are an entertainer, lecturer, or preacher. In any case, much of your impact on any audience will come from the amount of preparation you have made, and how well you respect and size up your audience.

In any case, you need your audience -- even if it appears to be the source of fear, the stage fright, which makes you want to flee them. The reason is simple. They give back, and they remake us. "It is hard," said pianist Arthur Rubinstein, "for us to get away from the wish to be applauded -- to charm and seduce."

Seeing the Audience
All of us who work, who produce goods or services, face an audience of sorts -- those who would buy or judge our work. But the performer has a special problem: his or her work is produced and seen at precisely the same time. In other areas of the arts, such as painting, writing and composing -- solitary endeavors, all -- the audience sees only the result of the creation. In any kind of live presentation, the

audience is present <u>during</u> the process.   And we are
acutely aware of this fact.

Part of the reason we are all so susceptible to
stage fright is that we see the audience as something
hostile, something pitiless and unknown.   So long as
you imagine the spectator-performer relationship as one
of judge and defendant, it's hard <u>not</u> to panic.   The
audience becomes the Grand Inquisitor, and you feel
threatened, terrified, isolated as a lone individual
pitted against a harsh sea of strangers.   But that is,
in almost all instances, a projection of our fears.   We
narcissistically turn the audience into a gigantic
mirror and in reality we are focusing upon ourselves,
judging ourselves as harshly as Torquemada.

Another way to view the audience, though, is to
perceive one's performance as an act of communication,
one in which neither party is being judged, but one in
which both are participating.   At the same time, we
benefit when we see performance as an act of giving, of
giving to our listeners something greater than our egos
-- something that makes self-preoccupation seem
trivial.   The greater your desire to give fully and the
less you think about being praised, the freer you will
be.

Said yet another way, some actors, such as the
late teaching great, Lee Strasberg, view the audience
as a partner.   In her chapter "Practical Problems,"
from her book <u>Respect for Acting</u>, actress-teacher Uta
Hagen poses this question: "How do I talk to the
audience?   I am not talking to myself, the audience is
my partner.   For students of Uta Hagen, this team mate,
the audience, must be made as specific as any other
character with whom there is a dialogue in a play.
This partnership is described by the improvisory clown

and mime, Avner Eisenberg. "The audience," he said, "is my partner. I have the scenario and we fill in the bits together." It is, in some sense, like any other human interchange.

Paradoxically, the more sensitive the performer is to the audience, the more likely he or she will succumb to feelings of fear. But there, too, is the reward. In many instances, good audience response stimulates a better performance. Performers say you know when the audience is with you, that there is a solid wave of feeling. Even with his back to the audience, conductor Michael Tilson Thomas says he can feel the vibrations. On the other hand, some actors resent their dependence on the audience and prefer to feel the presence of the other people on the stage, or simply perform with only their own words or their instrument. For these performers, the material being presented is the essential element; the audience takes on a less important role. One example is a clergyman who gives the impression of being so much absorbed in his spiritual message, that an audience seems almost an intrusion of his privacy. Most performers, however, are seeking appreciation and approval, and the audience embrace brings instant gratification.

The form of that embrace varies from wild applause to rapt appreciation. One view was voiced by the late Avon Long, who appeared in <u>Roots</u> and <u>Porgy and Bess</u>, and who danced at New York's famed Cotton Club in its heyday. "In fifty years," he said, "I've learned that what's better than applause is that profound silence of someone listening to you. That is the best. And the best I can give back is wanting to please. There are greater dancers, greater singers, greater actors, but there is nobody who wants to please like Avon, that's all I know."

It is not the performer alone who seeks gratification, of course. The audience, too, wishes more than a recitation of facts, notes or gestures; they want emotion, their own emotion. One dramatic example of this symbiotic relationship took place in New York City several years ago. After his final New York piano recital at the age of 89, the charismatic Arthur Rubinstein strode onto the stage. Audience response was overwhelming. "I love you," stated Mr. Rubinstein to an almost tearful audience, and the spontaneous cries came back, "We love you!" "The mortality of the interpreter's art and the mortality of the man were joined and, through the passing of some momentary beauty, the audience became aware of its own mortality as well."

It is more often a case of familiarity and warmth that makes the performer and audience one. Said the late James Coco, when acting in the Broadway cast of You Can't Take It With You, "Forget about the big black giant. I look upon the audience as just living breathing human beings. We get our vibes from them." And the director of this play, Ellis Rabb, remembers those wonderful nights -- the juncture of hundreds of people in the same room laughing together. "It's chemistry," he said, "that's what we are all working toward."

Reaching the Audience

The chemistry is not achieved easily. It is the result of a good deal of preparation, both of the material and of the speaker.

For myself, before a performance, I prepare myself musically, physically and psychologically, and when the curtain rises, I stand aside and allow the music to take over. I am not trying to win an audience, but to share with them, and as a consequence, I win. That is the "why" of my singing.

The end result of assiduous preparation will be, ironically, the illusion that what you are doing is natural, for audiences love naturalness. British actor Alec McCowen is certain that if you assembled Sir Laurence Olivier, Sir John Gielgud and all the foremost actors of the world upon a stage, and a cat wandered onto the stage, the audience would watch the cat. Why? "Because," said McCowen, "they don't know what the cat is going to do, the cat is natural." The hard work is trying to make the technique look natural and spontaneous so that each audience will feel it is witnessing a first time. Fortunately, although there is no fool-proof method for success before an audience, there are a number of techniques and experiences which move the odds considerably more in your favor.

Speak so that your audience will never dream that you are formally trained. A good speaker is like a window -- letting light in but not attracting attention to its source. Actor Kurt Russell says that you can create an illusion so well that the audience thinks it is seeing reality. This is how a good speaker, statesman, or performer throws attention away from himself and has the audience concentrate on what is presented. The performer's illusion becomes the audience's reality.

In his book, You Can Speak in Public, John Wolfe shares secrets about his podium prowess. The only way to be comfortable in front of an audience, says Wolfe, is to know what you're talking about. As long as you are prepared, he maintains, you can expect success --

although the exact response of the audience naturally varies.

To be prepared is not simply getting our lines or facts straight, it is also believing in your material. But the key to belief is practice. A well-prepared speech is already nine-tenths delivered. In this case, talking to yourself is not a form of madness but good planning. Act out the whole situation and concentrate on making the whole pre-enactment as realistic as possible. A talk is a voyage and must be charted. With material in hand, dress suitably for the occasion, and whenever possible, do a final review -- a dry run in the place, or kind of place, in which you will actually be speaking: a church, lecture hall, a hospital auditorium. Prior to the dry run, practice your message and practice slowly. You cannot do anything well that you cannot do slowly. Act out the entire talk at home, imagining it actually happening. This reduces an element of surprise which, in turn, reduces your anxiety.

No matter how realistic your preparations, however, you will experience a moment of shock when you are actually confronted with a live audience. Fear of public speaking is the most common social phobia. At this point, it will be important to take a moment to feel grounded in the situation. Look at the audience not as a sea of strangers, but as a group of human beings. Look at their eyes and observe their responses. If you have prepared your speech properly, you will need a minimum of notes. Although it's true that Lincoln read the Gettysburg Address, few talks longer than that will bear a reading. Working from notes you need not push your message, but trust that it will flow. Remember that when you begin, do so with the assumption that your audience really wants to hear from you. Much of the anxiety comes from the assumption that the audience will judge the speaker negatively. The speaker must realize that the audience does not have the power to hurt him. He must be convinced that he can enjoy his own performance; that he cannot control anyone else, and that if the performance is not his best, it can still be worthwhile.

There are a number of ways in which to make that important connection with the audience. For instance, you can choose someone in the audience representative of the entire audience. This can make the audience connection and the presentation organic and successful. It is a way of thinking which takes away from self-consciousness.

From the actor's point of view, there are three general ways to approach the audience: 1) perform directly to them, or 2) instead to your imaginary partner, projecting him or her into the audience itself or 3) onto the stage beside you. The second technique creates the illusion that you are performing to the audience directly, while the third casts the audience as an invisible witness who -- like the viewer of Degas' keyhole drawings -- has been given a secret glimpse of your most private, personal life. The first technique projects you into the audience's world; the second draws them into yours. Some people prefer to combine the two approaches, focusing alternatively on the audience and on a point nearby where they have conjured up an imaginary partner.

Although the techniques of stage acting differ in some respects from ordinary speechmaking, the same lesson is crucial: do not deny the existence of the audience. If you choose to do so, you will expend a good deal of unnecessary energy in denial. A seasoned performer can remain utterly involved with his imaginary world and still respond with the greatest sensitivity to every nuance of feeling his audience transmits -- just as an experienced driver can carry on an uninterrrupted conversation yet never stop adjusting the wheel or the gas in response to changes in traffic and topography.

It is by these very practiced forms of forgetting one's self that we are able to project ourselves best on stage. In other words, leave yourself alone and you will emerge. In addition, this lack of self-consciousness will enable you to move beyond, to take risks. As poet Robert Frost once noted, "The people I want to hear about are the people who take risks."

That time when the performer takes risks is a moment of excitement for the audience: the high notes of the singer; the almost impossible leap of the dancer or gymnast; the soliloquy of the actor; the closing arguments of the attorney; the climax of the sermon; the final pitch of the salesman. These moments are climactic not only because the script says so, or because it is physically difficult. It is also the time when the performer allows part of his concealed world, his interior, to be exposed. In that moment of performance, there is absolutely no room for anything else and if one misses its potential, it is gone. The celebrated operatic soprano Leontyne Price believes that giving the audience "an emotional experience is your reason at the moment for being alive."

But it is just such an exposure that we most fear, as it is just such an exposure that we seek. Because it is at this time that we give and get the most from our audience. It is also the time that we keep in the back of our heads, the time when the safety net of practice vanishes. We are out on the stage all alone, and it is from this moment, or fear of this moment, that stage fright appears to grow. But in fact, it begins long before that, and this is what we must explore.

CHAPTER 3

THE CONFLICT WITHIN

Stage fright hits like a ton of bricks. "I don't know what happened to me!" students will tell me. "I just lost it completely."

In actuality, however, panic grows from a slight ripple to an enormous paralyzing tidal wave by setting off a chain reaction that completely disconnects you from your feelings and your knowledge. You feel a twinge of anxiety at first. But instead of rising above this anxiety or stepping outside it, you begin to anticipate failure, clearly visualizing and even experiencing it. And before you know it, you are certain you are going out to face an enemy rather than walking onstage before a group of people who actually want to hear your message.

This sensation triggers a series of mental, emotional and physical responses which begin to further incapacitate you and creates a seemingly inexorable helplessness, a domino theory of reactions from which there is no escape. Mentally, you become self-conscious, worried about how you will appear to the audience, how you will do, rather than focused on what you are doing. Locked in, your senses are shut off.

You can't possibly concentrate on the character you are playing, the speech you are giving, or the music you are performing. You're a mess!

Off-balanced and out of control, your adrenalin soars to dangerous levels. The heart beats wildly and you fight for breath. As you struggle to brace yourself against the "danger" at hand, the body tenses up, muscles locking into place, to the point which you are unable to move. Now you've worked yourself into a state where you really aren't capable of expressing yourself at all.

As the fear of failure escalates, another cycle is set into motion, making the prospect of disaster more real, even greater:

-Anticipation of danger and potential failure

-Anxiety

-Self-consciousness

-Physical paralysis

Blocked off from your technical skills, you have no control over your body or thoughts. Failure becomes a self-fulfilling prophecy. What has happened is a chain of reactions, one which has many beginnings and many aspects. What I would like to do is show you a number of ways to look at it and, more importantly, to deal with it.

Stress

Stage fright is a stress reaction. According to Dr. Hans Selye, a pioneer in life stress research, the pounding heart, the turbulent stomach, the shaking hands, the fluttering butterflies are all the body's call to arms, the nervous system's sounding a state of red alert. Why? The stimulus is fear and the motive is survival.

It is, of course, in response to stress that stage
fright first appears, and the first instinct is to
defeat stress. One of the simplest responses would be,
then, not to appear on stage. But I presume that you
have read this far because you want to appear in front
of other people and you want to learn to cope with
stage fright.

Stress need not be a villain. Too often, it
evokes a negative image, one which obscures its
positive uses. Dr. Selye defines stress as "any demand
(internal or external) placed upon the organism or
person, that requires an adaptation to be made."[1]

It is impossible to live life and not be subject
to stress. And if properly channeled, stress reactions
can become the performer's greatest tool, bringing
about increased sensibility and endurance. For our
purposes, it is helpful to make the distinction which
Dr. Selye makes. Our reaction to stress takes two
forms: distress and eu-stress. Distress is a negative
response that can range from discouragement to despair.
Eu-stress is a natural constructive and adaptive
response. The most vivid example of this positive
potential can be seen in the relationship between
stress and performance. After losing a tennis match,
Chris Evert Lloyd once said: "I knew I was in trouble
when I didn't feel anxious." The truly inspired
performer has a "tensiveness" about him, an excitement,
a keyed-upness, like the energy stored in a coiled
spring. Athletes, opera singers, dancers, trial
lawyers, salesmen, teachers, even dinner party hosts

---

[1]Hans Selye, M.D., <u>Stress Without Distress</u> (McGraw
Hill, N.Y. 1975)

and hostesses, warm up, or psych up, before curtain time. Emotions during this period before action will naturally move toward a higher pitch, and we ought not fear this exhilaration. This onset of primitive energy, a survival instinct, is an inescapable part of each of us. It provokes a basic biological reaction called the fight or flight response. This is a hormonally stimulated state of arousal (hormones come from the Greek, hormao, meaning I arouse to activity) which prepares us for urgent action.

For performers, actually increasing the eu-stress level is developing an optimal level in order to enhance the best performance. This use of stress is what Dr. Victor Pease, author of Anxiety into Energy, calls "the stress window."

When we find our own stress window, we can play better tennis, sing better and even become better lovers. Through our stress window, senses and mind powers are sharpened, but the price we pay is heightened anxiety. Writer and pianist Seymour Bernstein believes, "Moreover, the wondrous playing of such artists as Arthur Rubinstein and Gregor Piatigorsky derives more from their ability to channel their nervous energy than from the maneuvers they take to allay its effects."

Dr. Pease emphasizes, "our stress reactions are designed to promote our survival, not to end it." Although each of us suffers an individual set of stress symptoms, we are all endowed with this formidable emotional resource. Make no mistake about it. We're all going to be "sized up" at our next job interview. We are entitled to be nervous. Then ask yourself, what is the worst thing that could happen -- another job interview, another opportunity.

Heightened tension, when properly channeled, can imbue the performance with an extended, mercurial shimmer -- an effervescence. To an actor who explained how he tried to "rid" himself of his nervousness, stage and opera director Frank Corsaro replied, "Yes, but you threw away the very thing that would have helped you. You must use your nervousness to show us this character. If you plan what you will show us, and repress everything else, you become conventional."

The trick is to make your nerves work for you instead of against you, and this, although no easy task, can be done. In the end, you can MAKE THOSE BUTTERFLIES FLY IN FORMATION.

The Way Out

As we see, stage fright is both a mental and physical response to performance stress. Mentally, it takes the form of intense anxiety and creative constipation. Physically, it is manifested as extreme hypertension, shortness of breath and a frightening, debilitating muscular paralysis. As Lear says in Shakespeare's great tragedy:

"We are not ourselves when nature, being oppressed, command the mind to suffer with the body."

To liberate one's self from this problem, you must know how to deal with, in fact, three aspects of stage fright: mental, physical and spiritual. Research has revealed that by changing your mental outlook the physical condition of many illnesses can be improved, and this extends to conditions such as stage fright. At the same time, changing one's physical condition will alter you mentally and emotionally. As the Romans said, "mens sana in corpore sano," a sound mind in a sound body. To this I must add the concept of spirituality, the recognition that there is a power greater than ourselves and our willingness both to use and be used by that power. Although many people may have trouble with such a concept, I find that it works for me and that if you are able, you may find that it will work for you.

Principally, however, the following chapters will reveal a regimen, one which you can adapt to your own needs and preferences, which will teach you skills for releasing tension and using tension. We will do this by:

1. Limbering up the body with physical excercise and stretching.

2. Centering physically through a combination of isometric and imaging techniques based on yoga.

3. Learning to breathe deeply and correctly.

Like the dancer's barre or the singer's scale, each relaxation technique should become daily routine. Continual practice will lend the mastery needed to implement these techniques when performance stress strikes. Daily practice will transform you into a more relaxed person, highly energized, yet free of excess tensions, centered, and deeply calm.

Real progress can only occur gradually -- seven hours in one day won't achieve as much as the same seven hours distributed over a two-week period. Be patient. Have the capacity of calm endurance. Don't set a time limit for reaching any given level of relaxation. Remember, you are learning how to release tension and center yourself, a process, rather than trying to achieve a particular level of relaxation, a finished product.

Be sure as you go along to focus on the process, not the results. Stay centered by accepting whatever you are doing. Mastery takes place in terms of "active passivity," i.e. through increased awareness and understanding. And begin modestly. Do not make extravagant promises to yourself or overestimate what you will accomplish on the first day. George Sheehan, M.D., the running guru, points out in his book, How to Feel Great 24 Hours a Day, that being born again means crawling before you walk, walking before you run. Begin now by taking that first step.

For those of you willing to use additional spirituality in your regimen, I'd like to briefly explain the concept. When the performer is in the correct frame of mind he or she is willing to be used by something greater than the self. The power is not reserved for performers of course; anyone can discover it in the course of daily life. What we are talking about is cultivation of faith, an act which evolves at the same time we are cultivating our commitment, confidence and internal discipline.

People of proven excellence know that if they don't believe in themselves, no one else will believe in them. Self-confidence is not unspiritual; quite the contrary, it is the honest belief in your own gifts and abilities. The faith factor, one's deepest personal beliefs, can enable you to draw on power beyond yourself.

In a lifetime of appearing before audiences, Dr. Norman Vincent Peale discovered the value of prayer. Dr. Peale, always self-conscious before an audience, prayed for courage and clarity of mind. "I have never," he said, "stood in the wings of an auditorium or in a pulpit in church without offering a prayer in which I send out love thoughts to the people in the audience or congregation." In every human being there

are universal feelings, that primal force. Sharing
these, although frightening and at times difficult, is
a celebration. The most realistic self-image is to
think of yourself as created in God's image, as are we
all. Then you will experience a deeper sense of
strength before appearing in front of strangers. To
share an experience, to reach and enlarge the
consciousness of another human being, is within reach
of us all. For some of us, we must fight the fear,
sometimes paralyzing fear, that stands in the way. But
that can make the rewards even greater, the experience
even more meaningful. So let us begin.

PART II

PROJECTING TOWARD SUCCESS

CHAPTER 4

CREATING YOUR OWN POSITIVE EMOTIONAL LANDSCAPE

"What you see is what you get."
                              -Flip Wilson

"Get your mind set in the groove it should
    follow."
                              -a Fortune Cookie

"Imagination is the health of every man."
                              -Ralph Waldo Emerson

In his book <u>The Hero with a Thousand Faces</u>, Joseph
Campbell talks about the almost magical ease with which
fairy tale heroes accomplish their appointed task.
Princesses melt at the sight of them; birds, chipmunks,
old woodcutters all throng to their aid; dragons fall
dead at one glance of their sword. The answer they
give to a riddle -- without even pondering -- is always
the right answer. There's an ease, a confidence, an
aura about them that makes everyone know they're going
to succeed -- to win the battle, win the kingdom, find
the secret for success, wealth, happiness and eternal
life. Ease signifies that the hero is a superior man,
a born king. Such heroes are among the chosen, the
blessed, the superman of this world. Fortune smiles on

them.   They are winners.   And they know they are winners.

Similarly, all truly great performers have an almost magical radiance, a spellbinding intensified aliveness about them.   They may be utterly unprepossessing in their daily lives but once on stage energy seems to pour out of them -- and pour out effortlessly.   For such people, the stage is the place where for a few precious moments they can live out the moments of their lives on a higher plane, they can release all they have to give.   Here is where they long and live to be.

Like religious celebrants, they celebrate life and its meaning through their art before other human beings who will share in it, be moved by it, transformed by it.   Performance is a time of ecstasy and joy for them. It is an opportunity to share and give of all that they know is in them.   The role they are about to play, the speech they are prepared to give, is not something separate from themselves which they must struggle to meet or match.   They are one with it, they are like a vessel through which the emotions, conception or shape pour.

Charles Garfield,[1] doctor of psychology and mathmatics, describes how Russians report that during moments of peak performance the athlete is apparently released from conscious thought processes and goes on automatic pilot.   "The athletes felt consumed by the momentum of the event itself.   They felt as though they were acting automatically, their minds and bodies like instruments perfectly tuned to the moment.   They participated in the action without conscious thought."

---

[1]Charles Garfield, Ph.D.   Peak Performance

And again: "An important part of the subjective experience of peak performance is a sense of ecstasy or joy. There is no more precious moment in life than this."

Many athletes refer to such moments as a cocoon of concentration and experience, what Lars-Eric Unestahl, Swedish sports psychologist, has called "the winning feeling," a feeling that you and the action you are performing are all that exist in the world. Massive reserves of energy, not ordinarily available, are released. One feels potent, right, utterly centered.[2] Once you learn to plug into this state of being when you perform on a regular basis, you can truly use all your potential and your stage fright will disappear.

You may still feel a certain amount of anticipatory anxiety but this is positive anxiety -- eu-stress -- which will arouse and activate you. Some degree of stimulation is essential. It is, of course, when stimulation goes beyond one's ability to control or accept that stage fright occurs, an event so traumatic that you can become completely terrified of its happening again.

We recall how it happens. As the date of each upcoming public appearance nears, your fear of an attack escalates. You may be gripped by anxiety every time you sit down to study or practice, or even so much as think about your next engagement. Such secondary "fear of fear" can impede technical mastery, erode all confidence, and make every prospective appearance too terrifying to contemplate. You then go onstage an unbalanced, tense human being and disaster is likely to ensue.

---

[2] Charles Garfield, Ph.D. Peak Performance.

People, I believe, often have a misconception about fear and courage: courage is being scared and overcoming it. And overcoming does not, unfortunately, mean conquering or subduing fear so that it never strikes again. A life without fear is about as likely as a life without pain -- no life at all. But within you is the power to succeed, to do things you never dreamed possible. The question is, how to reach that power, and how to break the cycle of fear?

This is where creative visualization comes in. Creative visualization, much as the name implies, is a method for establishing positive images within, ones which enhance our abilities and self-image. According to its developer, Shakti Gawain, it is "a technique for using your imagination to create what you want in life ... fulfillment, enjoyment ... rewarding work, self-expression, health, beauty, prosperity, inner peace and harmony." Practitioners of the technique may use it to get in touch with their own inner potency, imbue their craft with love, a sense of excitement, and finally to use it to see their performing as a celebration of their own vitality, rather than a cauldron of negativity and fear.

Moreover, as you begin to visualize creatively, you begin to discover what inner blocks and fears, if any, are locking you into a pattern of fearfulness and negativity and, as these begin to surface, to let them go.

If you make creative visualization a part of your life, you may begin to experience amazing results in terms of both the subjective and objective quality of your performances. This in turn will fortify your confidence and sense of power. Creative visualization can also help you to transform your self image as well as your vision and experience of what it means to perform. With practice you can reprogram your mind so that you begin to approach your work in an entirely new and exciting way.

We all use our imaginations to visualize every day, every hour, every minute -- most of us unconsciously. Unfortunately, so many of us -- phobic people in particular -- spend most of their time imagining what might go wrong, visualizing obstacles, dangers, potential disasters and embarrassing failures. We fill our minds with pictures of what we fear might happen, and so failure becomes the only thing of which we have a clear picture. Unconsciously, by such patterns we are creating the very thing we fear the most, failure. To succeed, to be a winner, you must first have a clear picture of what success feels like and involves: this picture can guide your efforts to program yourself for peak performances.

The power of creative visualization is enormous. Almost every star performer uses it whether consciously or intuitively. Says Olympic Gold medalist Bruce Jenner: "I have always felt my greatest ability was not my physical ability, it was my mental ability." And the former Mr. Universe, Arnold Schwarzenegger testifies: "All I know is that the first step is to create the vision because when you see the vision, there, the beautiful vision, that creates the 'want' power. My wanting to be Mr. Universe came about because I saw myself so clearly being up there on the stage and winning."

The Soviets have made imaging a crucial part of the training process for their Olympic teams. Having "discovered" that emotional stresses such as anxiety and self-doubt can be extremely detrimental in competition, they developed techniques to teach their athletes to run detailed mental tapes of ideal moves, strategies, etc. These moves were gone over again and again during mental rehearsals until the athletes were virtually "programmed" for success. They had created neuromuscular templates of an ideal high jump or dive which would automatically guide them during the actual competitions. At the same time, Swedish sports psychologist Lars-Eric Unestahl has worked extensively with a similar technique called "hypnotic goal programming" in which he teaches atheletes to put themselves into a deeply relaxed mental state and then create pictures of their goals.

Writes American poet Charles Siebert, describing how Olympic athletes attain such amazing levels during performance: "much of the story occurs prior to the event -- they remain out of sight, honing their skills and concentration, and then emerging for one or two moments of the extreme execution during which their picture either coalesces or crumbles." And, says Jack Nicklaus in Golf My Way: "I never hit a shot, not even in practice, without having a sharp and focused picture of it in my head. It's like a color movie. First I see the ball where I want it to finish. Then the scene quickly changes and I see the ball going there: its path, trajectory and shape, even its behavior on landing. Then...the next scene shows me making the kind of swing that will turn the previous energy into reality...Visualizing the swing is useless unless you visualize what it is supposed to achieve."

People who imagine shooting basketballs through a hoop were better than a control group who had no mental practice. Actual practice is important. Visualization is no substitute for practice. You learn a skill by physically practicing it; learning to "see and feel" yourself moving with the basketball also requires practice. With concentrated effort you can learn these strategies.

Creative artists also spend a great deal of time visualizing -- though not always in strictly visual terms. Musicians work hard to develop their "inner ear" -- the capacity to hear sound in their heads. Says singer Jessye Norman: "Singing takes place in the brain." The vocal cords do only what they are told to do. The more you practice visualization the easier it will become. Here are some techniques to help you visualize creatively.

To teach yourself the basics of creative visualization, choose some event, object or situation you want to have happen in your life: owning a new car, some new clothes, a new job, a trip to the Riviera, making love to someone wonderful, etc. Stay away from specific performance-related goals for now, though, because they may be more difficult for you to visualize. Later, using the same techniques, you can substitute your particular area of performance. But for now, choose a goal that is simple and easily conceivable, making sure it's something you really want.

HOW TO DO IT
1. Relax. Or more accurately, begin to relax. In practice, use the yogic deep relaxation response or any other method you feel comfortable with to sink into this state. Inhale thinking "re" and exhale thinking "lax."

According to Shakti Gawain: "... when your body and mind are deeply relaxed, your brain wave pattern

42

actually changes and becomes slower. This deeper, slower level is commonly called the alpha level (while your usual busy waking consciousness is called beta level).... It has been found to be far more effective than the more active beta level in creating real changes in the so-called objective world, through the use of visualization." Fortunately, the human nervous system cannot differentiate betweeen the real experience and the imagined one. An imagined stimulus can stand in for an observed one producing an effect that is indistinguishable from actual perception.[3]

Deep relaxation, then, is achieved through visualization. We picture a wave of blue or gold or whatever flowing up over our bodies and picture each part of the body relaxed as well -- and it does! The same is true if you picture your body as filled with sawdust and imagine the sawdust to be seeping out, first from your toes, your ankles, etc. Being aware of the power of the imagination keys you into the ability of the mind to transform physical reality through imaging.

2. Create a picture. Once you feel truly relaxed and your mind is quite still (you are in a semi-meditative state), imagine what you want exactly the way you would like it to be. If it's an object, see yourself using it -- for example if you choose a satin gown, see yourself wearing it, feel the softness of the cloth, see people admiring you. If it's a car, imagine driving it, enjoying it. If it's a situation or event, picture yourself there and everything happening just

---

[3]Mental Imagery Ability, Stephen M. Kosslyn, from Human Abilities, edited by P.J. Sternberg, W.H. Freeman and Co., 1985.

the way you want it to. You may want to imagine the people around you, hear what they are saying. Sensory aspects of the experience -- like sound, touch, taste and smell -- will often help make the experience seem even more real and sensuous to you.

Texture your image. If you are visualizing yourself on a beach, for example, you may want to include details like the texture of the sand under you body, the feel of suntan lotion being massaged into your body by someone who excites you, the feel of the sun caressing your back, rain forests and sea air, the sound of waves rippling on the beach or of exotic birds of paradise. Include whatever details make the picture more real and more provocative for you. Have fun with this. Enjoy it the way a child enjoys daydreaming. Easily make the pictures come to life in your imagination. Don't try to hold on to any details or sensations either. Let them come and go freely.

3. Affirm. Once you have enjoyed this for a while and feel complete, with the picture still in your mind make some positive statement affirming that it has really taken place. Something like:

I am the new owner of a BMW. Everyone is dazzled by it. I will drive it to all sorts of exciting places.

I am now climbing in the Grand Tetons. It is clear and dry, my pack feels light and I feel strong.

I am now enjoying a wonderful vacation on a fascinating tropical island. I am having an exciting and thoroughly enjoyable time.

Affirmations, according to Shakti Gawain, who leads workshops on creative visualization, imbue your visualizations with positive energy and strengthen your belief in their possibility. Ms. Gawain also recommends ending each visualization with this statement:

This or something better now manifests for me in totally satisfying and harmonious ways, for the highest good of all concerned.

These words prevent you from attaching too much importance to everything happening exactly the way you imagined it to. They permit you to live in the moment, trusting that, if you do so, life may offer you unexpected and wonderful surprises.

For example, a public speaker visualizing his speech going exactly the way he would like it, but allowing for something better, though unexpected, will not be thrown by an unanticipated question from the audience. Rather he will see it as an opportunity to experience something even richer than what he'd visualized in his mind's eye.

The words also remind you that what you are creating in your life will be good for you and all concerned. To help that along, always spin a successful ending to your visualizations. Negative feelings and images, conversely, will sabotage visualization. The mind is like a garden capable of planting positive or negative thoughts. You can apply this same basic technique toward actualizing goals connected with your work.

At the same time, don't worry about whether you are visualizing "the right way." Whatever you are doing, whatever works for you so that you are caught up in your fantasy as a daydream, whatever enhances your belief in yourself -- this is the right way for you. Experiment with conscious statements that work for you. Use whatever works best, and remember that people differ in the quality and kind of imagery they can use.

The more you fill your picture with sensory impressions, however, the more vividly it will imprint itself on your brain. In her book, Soprano In Her Head, Eloise Ristead talks about feeling bodily reactions in your imagination: she refers to "a feeling sense." When you are really caught up in a visualization, this feeling sense is activated -- your body begins to feel the heat of the tropics, the ocean breeze, the sensation of whirling around a dance floor just as if you were actually doing it. This in turn activates the emotions -- and you find yourself feeling the accompanying peacefulness, elation or exhilaration, etc.

A visualized picture is like a delicate flower. If you try to pry it open you will destroy it. Do not try to force anything -- if a particular detail doesn't coalesce for you, let it be. Take all the time you need! Quite often a picture will fluctuate in intensity. It may suddenly seem to be fading, losing its hold on your imagination. That's perfectly natural and if it happens, stop for a moment, take a deep breath and go back. Let the images flow. Go only with what appeals to you.

There are actually two kinds of visualizing: active and passive. In active visualization, we consciously select the picture we want to see, and build it accordingly. Rather as a painter might say to himself, "Now I'm going to paint a girl and she'll have on a ... pink ... dress" and he makes a conscious choice to make the dress pink. In passive visualization, on the other hand, we simply relax and allow images to pass through our minds. Effective creative visualization involves a combined use of active and passive imaging. You begin actively, but as you proceed details may begin to suggest themselves spontaneously. Go with these suggestions. Sometimes you may even choose something consciously, but your inner voice suggests something else. For example, as you start to imagine a resort in Hawaii, a walk through a desert in bloom may suggest itself. Go with this; it is the voice of the unconscious, your inner guide advising you. This inner guide is often more in touch with what you really want and dream of than your conscious mind.

You may, in fact, want to ask your inner guide questions, such as: "What does the desert sun feel like on my body?" And then, open yourself to receive the answer. Try not to think it up, but rather let your body find the feeling. For instance, ask, "What does water sound like?" And let your ears find this sound. Once your ears find the sound of the water, they may begin to hear other sounds as well: the rustling of palm trees, etc. You may want to offer gentle suggestions to your imagination, but if you jump to come up with details instead of letting them happen, you may lose touch with the spontaneous flow of images.

Simone Weil, in her book, <u>Waiting For God</u>, describes creative attention as "negative effort." Said she:

"Attention consists of suspending our thought, leaving it detached, empty, and ready to be penetrated by the object...all wrong translations...all faulty connections... are due to the fact that thought has seized upon some idea too hastily, and being thus prematurely blocked, is not open to the truth. The cause is always that we have wanted to be too active, we have wanted to carry out a search."

Throughout the ages, men have been aware of an inner center, which is the source of all true creative inspiration, and which, if you connect to it and listen to it, it will direct you towards those goals that are right for you -- that will fulfill and enrich your life and others.

Modern man has become so enamored of the idea that the individual "makes his own life happen" through conscious effort and struggle in a hostile, ultimately senseless world, through the sheer force of his will, has isolated himself from those very life energies, that psychic connection that could give his goals and strivings a feeling of <u>rightness</u>. If, during creative visualization, you combine your active imaging with listening to the voice of your own "inner center" as it manifests through spontaneous suggestions -- passive imagery -- your goals as they are pictured will end up feeling much more "right." You will feel as though they have been <u>revealed</u> to you quite as much as <u>created</u> by you. As if the voice of your own desire and the intent of whatever you believe in are one. And your sense of connection to an inner center, as well as your sense of being part of a larger pattern, will deepen.

To Enhance Visualization

1. <u>Include movement</u>. Still pictures are not enough; moving pictures are better. That's why it's so important to imagine yourself using a desired object, showing it to your friends, etc. Or doing, moving in a situation you may want to have happen in our life. Always include yourself in the visualization.

2. <u>Try as much as possible to believe your picture is
real while you meditate on it</u>. Don't push for belief.
At the same time try not to let your intellect censor
it. There is a kind of belief in fantasies, or movies
-- a suspension of disbelief, actually -- that children
have very easily. And it comes from letting yourself
go with your feelings, be in the moment and not
watching or judging yourself. Don't criticize
yourself. Rather, accept yourself and build on that.

3. <u>Dealing with blocks and doubts</u>. Occasionally,
someone will have an enormous resistance to
visualization. If this happens, it's because he has
some sort of fear, generally connected often to fear of
failure, fear of success -- or having to do with the
particular thing he's visualizing that he doesn't want
to face. The best thing in such a case is to allow
whatever negative thoughts, feelings and images are
connected to the visualizing to present themselves; to
stay with these feelings for a while; and then to "let
them go."

Even someone who is not completely blocked as a
visualizer, however, may have feelings of doubt,
anxiety, dread, arise during a visualizing session.
Once again, the best thing is not to censor anything
that drifts into your mind while you visualize. Simply
observe the doubt or fear, and let it float out as it
will if you do not cling to it.

In general, if you allow yourself to dwell with
the feeling for a while, you often discover what it's
really about and this quite often cancels it.
Moreover, if you learn to allow such feelings to float
in and out -- recognize them -- they lose much of their

potency. It's not a fear <u>per se</u> that's most destructive to a performer, but rather denial of or fear of that fear.

Begin now to picture yourself before an audience. Remember the person you see in your imagination will always rule your world. See yourself stepping forward with confidence. Listen to the hush fall upon the room as you begin. Feel the attentive absorption of the audience as you drive home point after point. Feel the warmth of the applause as you leave the platform and hear the words of appreciation as they greet you when the meeting is over. Believe me, this is magic -- the never to be forgotten thrill.

CHAPTER 5
AFFIRMATIONS FOR PEAK PERFORMANCE

Affirmations

Affirmations (to make firm) are powerful statements that strengthen your belief that what you visualize can happen. To get the most our of creative visualizations, you should do affirmations frequently throughtout the day; speak them out loud, to yourself, or write them down.   Do whatever you feel more comfortable with.

Although you will be making simple declarative statements of hope, know that when you do your affirmations you aren't trying to change what is, but are creating new possibilities in your life. Each moment of your life is utterly new, unique among all those moments that preceded it. Affirmations give you a chance to feel how the moment you are living now can be different from the moment you lived yesterday, an hour ago. The present moment is the only reality.

The following are sample affirmations prepared by Shakti Gawain.   You may use these or create some of your own.

1. Every day, in every way, I am getting better and better.

2. Everything I need is already within me.
3. I love and appreciate myself just as I am.
4. I accept all feelings as part of myself.
5. It's OK for me to have everything I want.
6. When I perform, I surrender myself
    effortlessly to the beauty of my work.

Choose affirmations that are right for you, that feel stimulating, inspiring, expansive, empowering. Some people find declarations of selfhood best, such as affirmation #3. Others find metaphorical affirmations most effective: "When I speak or preach my spirit soars!"

In any case, the purpose of affirmations is to change our thoughts. The reason is simple: according to the ancient yogi, you become what you think. Most of us are aware of a continuous inner dialogue going on in our heads, commenting on how our lives are going, what we have to do tomorrow. The more you do affirmations, the more you begin to replace the present worrying, anxious chatter and old worn-out tapes of conversations past. Instead will come positive, confidence-building thoughts. Internal self-dialogue of a positive nature can take place when we answer the question, "How do I feel?" Make your self talk work for you.

Some rules concerning affirmations

1. <u>Always use the present tense</u>. Create what you want in your life as if it were already happening, not as if it will happen some indefinite time in the future.
2. <u>Always phrase affirmations in the most positive way you can</u>.
Although you may sometimes need to phrase affirmations negatively, do so in a positive way. For instance, I

said to myself, "I do not need to dwell on my years of inactivity." But I followed this with a simple, positive affirmation: "I am practiced, accomplished and ready."

3. <u>Keep your affirmations as strong, short and simple as possible</u>.

4. <u>Don't say your affirmations by rote</u>. Try to give yourself over to them, to listen and believe.

5. <u>Remember: You are not trying to change what exists in your life; you are trying to create something new and fresh</u>. This is enormously important. Paradoxically as it may seem, you must accept yourself the way you are before you can change. Self-doubt, fear that you aren't good enough, and unrealistic aspirations lie at the root of performance anxiety -- perhaps all anxieties. You must experience and acknowledge all feelings, even negative ones. Rather than deny or force negativity out, we are attempting to slowly, gently, give ourselves something better. To replace, one day at a time, the negative forces in our selves.

CHAPTER 6
SPIRITUALITY

Creative visualization, for many people, works that much better when we invoke spiritual sources, those ranging from the concept of God to spirit of the universe to specific masters.

It is not my intention to preach, nor to convert. But the fact is, for those afflicted with stage fright, a sense of the spiritual is more than helpful. Stage fright is, in a sense, a function of ego involvement. And, to the extent that you can experience yourself as empowered by something greater than yourself -- whether a divine being or force, or simply all humanity -- to that extent you will be greater able to experience yourself as a potent, radiant, and sure performer.

Affirmations referring to spiritual sources can create and deepen the connection to both a higher power, and between performer and audience. The writings of all those truly great performers and teachers who could move their audiences so deeply, reveal that they in a sense forgot about themselves and surrendered instead to their art. When they did, they left behind all ego-oriented concerns about success and failure the moment they began to perform.

It is not necessarily a religious connection,

either. The dancer Isadora Duncan -- an avowed athiest -- found her sense of purpose, her moving force, in the idea of reestablishing a connectedness to nature. Her sense of oneness with the cosmos, the universe, fed her, inspired her as a performer. Transmitting this sense gave her work its meaning.

Consider, too, the turn of the century Italian actress Eleanora Duse, perhaps the greatest who ever lived. Known to some as a spiritual figure, the 'doyenne' of the theatrical world, Eva La Gallienne called her the "mystic of the theater." A New York Times editorial published a day after her death asserted: "She transcended them all. Bernhardt and Coquelin, Irving, Mansfield, and Von Sonnethal ... the major part of Duse's art lay in a thing which no one could definitely see or adequately describe -- the thing for which we have only the poor, hackneyed word 'spirit'." Duse herself called it la Grazia, a kind of divine grace, to which she dedicated her life. "Nijinsky was known to the world as a great dancer -- the Dieu de la Danse -- but he was more. His aim was not to entertain or to reap success and glory for himself, but to transmit a divine message through his own medium -- the danse."

Performing and spirituality often go together, and is not, of course, limited to dancers and actors, great or otherwise. I could just as easily mention speakers like Martin Luther King, Clarence Darrow, great physicians, heads of government. You must find your own, be it secular or religious, and to use it along with affirmations and the rest of the following program. As I said, stage fright is but a symptom. What we are coming to terms with is fear, and the opposite of fear, and the antidote to fear is faith.

PART III

HARNESSING YOUR STRESS

REGIMENS

The following three chapters constitute a physical basis for dealing with anxiety in general, and aimed at stage fright in particular. Relaxation, centering, and breathing exercises, for many people, will also increase your abilities to work and play. They provide an active method of beginning to deal with fear.

CHAPTER 7

RELAXATION: "SHAKING OUT" AND "LIMBERING UP"

Studies of the most successful men and women today show that most engage in some kind of vigorous physical activity for at least 20 minutes a day. Such exercise uncramps the muscles, gets the blood flowing, lungs pumping, heart beating. Toxins and tensions accumulated during an arduous day flush out and you emerge feeling high: relaxed, cleansed, exhilarated.

Tennis, running, swimming, aerobic classes -- all can invigorate and leave you with a sense of energized calm. Incorporate 20 minutes to an hour of whatever form of aerobic exercise appeals to you into your day. Even a brisk walk can do wonders.

Stretching out is a must before and after a vigorous aerobic exercise period in order to warm up and cool down your muscle and organs to and from such a heightened level of activity. Otherwise you may wake up the next morning with serious cramps or muscle soreness which will cause more physical tension than you started out with.

If you don't have time for aerobics, a good round of shaking out when you wake up in the morning or come home in the evening can help undo some tension. Plan to devote 10 or 15 minutes to limbering-up once or twice a day. I guarantee that you'll feel the difference.

Posture

Remember that good posture is essential to productive stretching. When not standing with the stomach muscles pulled up firmly for support, you tend to compensate by gripping the shoulders, neck, upper and lower back to stay erect. When aligning the spine and using the stomach for support becomes a habit, you no longer need to compensate. Discover how to lift through the spine without tensing up, alert yet at ease. Good posture also instills confidence. In The King and I Anna sings, "Whenever I am afraid I hold my head erect so no one will suspect I'm afraid/The result of this deception is very strange to tell/Whenever I fool the people I fear I fool myself as well."

Stretching

To begin the stretch routine stand up straight, head forward and up, buttocks tucked under you and abdominal muscles pulled in and up against the spine.

Think of this as a lengthening and lifting rather than a "scrunching in." Drop your shoulders and lengthen your neck. Imagine an invisible string passes through the center of your body from your feet on up the legs and spine, continuing through the back of the neck and up on the top of the head, to a point on the ceiling directly above you. The string keeps lifting, lifting you up. Don't tilt your head up from the chin. The head is the last vertebra of the spine; it lifts because the entire spine and neck are lifting under it.

To check your alignment, stand with your back to a wall, shoulders touching the wall. If you are standing correctly the small of the back and back of the neck should touch the wall as well. Make this your goal.

Now move back to a comfortable location maintaining the alignment and shift weight forward over the balls of your feet. Get ready to shake, rattle and roll!

1) Head Rolls:
Let your head drop forward, jaw relaxed. Slowly drop your head to the right. Back, left. Forward. Keep it rotating continuously without pausing front, back or to either side. Don't resist the motion or try to hold your head in place. Let the movement take hold and exert no more effort than absolutely necessary to keep it going. You should feel as if someone has given your head a gentle push and it simply keeps rotating of its own accord.

Imagine that your head is rolling on top of, but independent of, your neck -- rather like a tether-ball rolling around and around atop a long pole. Your neck should feel as if it is elongating upward throughout the exercise, never "scrunching down.

The jaw should be relaxed throughout the exercise, dropping open as your head drops back and hanging "rag doll" to the side as your head begins to drop to the side.

Complete at least ten slow rotations.

Now begin to accelerate your rotations till your head feels like a spinning top whirling around and around. Or think of it as a star, spinning freely in space!

Reverse directions and repeat the exercise.

2) <u>Facial Relaxers</u>:
1. Face forward. Yawn a few times. With both thumbs supporting the base of the jaw, massage its hinges with your index fingers. This is done to "unlock" the jaw. Think of your fingers as conductors through which the jaw's tensions drain away.

2. Drop your jaw - unhinge, don't strain it open. Just let it go.

Now use your hands to move the jaw up and down and side to side, like the jaw of a nutcracker. Be sure that your <u>hands</u> are making the movement happen -- that the jaw isn't really moving itself. It should in fact be completely relaxed by now. As a test, take your hands away. If the jaw automatically drops open you're doing fine. If it remains "held" in a position there's still some tension here to drain away.

3. Massage your temples. If you feel any tension there, let it fall away. Rub your hands together, until they feel quite warm. Place palms over your closed eyes and allow

them to rest there until all warmth has
drained into the eyes. Stroke the closed
eyes gently a few times with your
fingertips.

3. Shake Outs:
Shoulders:
Shrug shoulders up. Hold for about 3 seconds.
Let them drop. (The rest of your body should
be still). Only the shoulders should move.
Repeat 10 times. Rotate your shoulders.
10 times forward. 10 times backward.

Arms:
Swing your right arm forward, up, round to the
back and down. Forward, up, round to the back
and down. The movement should be free and
loose -- a continuous swinging round and round.
Here again, use the least possible energy so
that it's happening from its own momentum.
Swing faster, faster! Just let your arm go.
Let it become part of the motion.

Repeat at least 20 times.

Reverse directions. Repeat at least 20 times.

Switch arms. Swing forward at least 20 times,
backward at least 20 times.

Now swing both arms forward together 20 times.
Backward together 20 times.

Shake out the arms.

Drop both arms down by your sides. Raise your
right hand to your chest, elbow extended to the
side. Throw the arm out to the side and let it
fall. Think of this as "throwing your arm
away." Throw it out from your center like a
ball and it extends and then falls of its own
accord. Don't hold on to it. Repeat 5 times.
Change arms and repeat 5 times. Once you
"eject" it, you lose control of it as it were.

Feet:
Sitting on the floor, extend your right foot
forward, leg straight and raised about 2 inches
off the ground. Rotate the foot 5 times to
the right, 5 times to the left. Make sure not
to move the calf at all -- the rotation starts
at the ankle! As you move your foot, keep the
toes as separate as possible. Feel the space
in between them.

Repeat the exercise with the left foot.

Legs:
Shake out your lower legs vigorously.

Swing the entire leg around free-form from the
hip joint. Feel a looseness - a freedom - in
this swing.

Hands:
With your elbows raised to the side and hands
in front of your chest, shake your hands out up

and down, as if you were waving goodbye. Shake
them faster! As fast as you can! Keep shaking
until they feel as if they're about to drop
off...and then shake some more.

4. Dropdowns:
   Your pace should be slow but steady in this
   exercise, determined by a deep even breathing
   pattern. Stabilize your breathing before
   beginning.

   1. With knees slightly bent, let the upper body
      drop forward, vertebra by vertebra. First
      let the head fall forward, let it hang as
      dead-weight. Then the neck. Then the next
      vertebra below the neck and so on, on down
      the spine. Note: Each "release" should be
      executed on an exhalation. Slightly below
      waist level (the point varies from
      individual to individual, depending on
      flexibility and weight), you will reach a
      point where you simply must drop the rest
      of the way down in a single motion until,
      ideally, your fingers touch the floor.
      Gravity will pull you down unless you
      resist. Don't resist! Let your torso drop
      the rest of the way down on a single
      exhalation.

   2. Breathing deeply, let yourself hang in this
      drop-down position: arms, head, jaw, neck,
      torso -- all dead-weight, all absolutely
      relaxed. Let your torso sway back and
      forth, side to side, like a rag doll's.

Hang centered for a while. Then begin to
swing again. From a centered position, lift
your head up to to the point of straining,
then let it fall. Repeat a few times. Sway
some more. Return to a simple hang
position.

3. To return to an upright position, straighten
up vertebra by vertebra beginning with the
lowest vertebra of the spine, that is,
"place" each vertebra directly on top of
the last, one at a time. The head is the
last to come up.

4. Repeat the drop-down as described above
several times. Eventually, when you become
secure and comfortable with the procedure,
add a series of about 10 rapid drop-downs,
dropping all the way down on a single
exhalation; return to an upright position on
a single inhalation. Make sure, however, to
drop down and rise up through the spine,
vertebra by vertebra, in the same way as
you did on the slower drop-downs, but now in
a single, flowing motion.

The serious student should think of these
exercises as an introduction only -- an introduction to
a full spectrum of tension-releasing stretch exercises.
There are many, many others -- some variations on the
same basic themes, some altogether different -- and you
can learn all about them in yoga and other
stretch-oriented classes. While these routines
described above work best for me (and I want you to

feel free to use them), I hope they inspire you to find out about some of these other exercises as well. Explore as much as possible; then put together a 10 minute program of your own.

Everyone carries his or her tension differently. For many people, tension lodges mainly in the neck and shoulders. For others, the lower back is the number-one trouble spot. Find out where your tensions tend to accumulate. Which stretches are hardest for you? Do you grimace involuntarily during the arm swings? Do you experience shoulder tension? Are you afraid to "let go" on the head rolls as your head drops to the back? (neck tension!). Do you have a difficult time dropping-down vertebra by vertebra when you get below chest level? In developing a routine, focus on your problem areas -- but don't ignore the rest of your body! Make sure your program is all-inclusive.

It's extremely important to know your own body, not just its weaknesses but its strengths as well. Think about how it feels as you stretch and shake, drop and swing your arms, legs and back. These preceding exercises will help you get to know your body and truly inhabit it, perhaps for the first time.

To further deepen your awareness and "at-homeness" in your body, try moving around free-form with your eyes closed to a piece of your favorite music. Discover how you can bend and twist. Think of the space around you as a viscous fluid and feel the shapes you make as you move through it. The better you come to know and enjoy your body, the more at one you will feel with it, and the more centered, comfortable and physically in control of yourself you will be in situations of stress.

CHAPTER 8
CENTERING

Once you roll and shake out your basic tensions it's time to prepare for <u>deep relaxation or centering</u>. Set aside at least 10, preferably 15 minutes a day following one of your stretch-outs for this process. It will prove well worthwhile.

Centering allows you to drain all tension from the body and promotes relaxation and restoration of energy. We return to a kind of womb-like calm, a state of consciousness without thought. Self-consciousness (in the literal sense of the word) disappears, along with all awareness of past or future. Separation between mind and body vanishes. You no longer feel as though you are in part watching yourself with an analytic eye from the outside in. You no longer watch yourself at all. You are simply immersed in "being." And you emerge from this state empowered by a strong sense of <u>inner connectedness</u>.

<u>Centering</u>

Find a quiet and comfortable relaxation hideout. Lie down on the floor, facing the ceiling, eyes closed, feet six inches apart, arms at your side. Don't exert

a single muscle to support yourself in this position,
just let go. Let yourself sink down into the floor.
The floor will support you. Breathe deeply and slowly
like an umbrella opening. Then let it go. Imagine you
are floating on a wide expanse of gently rippling
water.

    If you can't lie on the floor, sit upright in a
firm chair, eyes closed, hands at your side, feet on
the ground. In a state of complete relaxation, the
small of your back and back of your neck touch the
floor or chairback. Don't try to make this happen,
just let it happen. If you can't achieve total
relaxation right away, don't worry about it!
Everything will come in time. Be patient, and follow
these steps as best you can.

Tensing and Relaxing Different Muscle Groups:
You will begin by going over each part of the body
- pressing all the tensions within that part
together then expelling them entirely; maximum
tension followed by maximum release.

Legs and Arms:
Flex your right foot and extend your right leg,
tensing it as much as you can. Extend it. Extend
it. Lift it a couple of inches off the ground.
Tense it harder. Harder. Harder. Release it.
Shake it out. Forget about it. Do the same with
your left leg, now your right arm; making a fist
with your right hand; now your left arm.

Buttocks:
Squeeze your buttocks together - tighter, tighter,
tighter! Let them go. Forget about them.

Torso:
Breathing in through the nose, inflate your
stomach like a balloon. When you feel it's about
to burst, pump it even fuller. Hold the air in to
the count of 5. Now open your mouth and let all
the air out in one puff. Repeat, this time
inflating the rib cage and chest area, leaving the
abdomen completely relaxed.

Face:
Scrunch up your face as tightly as you can. Hold
for a count of 5. Let it go. Now stretch in the
opposite direction -- raising your eyebrows as
high as possible and opening your mouth as wide as
possible, sticking the tongue out so that it
reaches down for your toes. Hold for 5, stretching
more, more, more! Release.

Deep Release:
The next step in the centering process is based on
imaging techniques. No deliberate movement -- no
shaking, stretching or flopping -- is involved
here at all. Instead, you will put yourself into
a deep and refreshing state of relaxation (yogic
sleep) simply by imagining/feeling the parts of
your body relax, one by one. A wave of relaxation
as it were, will flow over you beginning at your
toes and moving up your legs, torso, etc. until
you are completely immersed in it.

Close your eyes. Breathe slowly and deeply.
Imagine smelling a rose. Begin now to allow all
cares and thoughts to fall away from the center of
your consciousness. Do not censor your thoughts.

Simply allow them to pass on through your mind.
Do not hold onto them. Contemplate them with
detachment. Let them go. Focus your attention on
the inner workings of your body; imagine your
heart relaxing -- chest relaxing -- stomach
relaxing -- everything relaxing. Now let your
attention rest for a minute or so on the rhythm of
your breathing. In, out. In, out. The yogic
word for breath, prana, means vitality, energy,
strength of life.

Now go over your body once more, feeling each of
its parts relax, one by one. (This process
requires intense mental alertness and
concentration but no mental strain. Do not try to
force the various parts of your body to relax.
Rather, experience/feel them relaxing. This
distinction may seem subtle, but it'scrucial.
Stay with each part for approximately one
inhalation and exhalation.

Feel your toes relax. Ankles. Calves. Knees.
Thighs. Hips. Genital area. Stomach. Rib cage.
Chest. Back. Shoulders. Neck. Jaw. Area
behind your ears. Feel your tongue wide and relax
in your mouth. Feel your teeth relax.

Feel your temples relax. Eyelids. Feel your
eyeballs relax in their sockets. Feel your
forehead relax. The top of your head. Feel your
brain relax.

Feel your upper arms relax. Elbows. Lower arms.
Wrists, palms. Back of your hands. Your fingers.

As you focus on each part of the body, direct your
breath (inhalation) toward it. Exhale through
that area and let all tension flow out of it with
the stream of your breath.

There are two alternative methods for achieving deep
release:

1) Imagine you are lying in a bed of warm sand and
   your body is filled with sand as well - or
   sawdust. As you focus attention on each of its
   parts, the sand or sawdust begins to seep out
   of you at that point as if out of a rag doll.
   The seeping sand mingles with the sand
   surrounding you. First your toes begin to go
   limp, then your ankles. And onward.

2) Choose a calming color -- sky blue, pale yellow
   or green, and imagine that a wave of this color
   is gently washing over your entire body. First
   it washes over your toes and you feel your toes
   relax. Not it is flowing over your ankles too,
   and you feel them relax, etc.

   After you have gone over the entire body,
   continue to breathe deeply and evenly. If you
   feel any remaining tensions anywhere, direct
   your breath toward that spot and release it.
   Once you feel completely relaxed, remain as you
   are for about 10 to 15 minutes longer. A
   wave of calm and tranquility will float under,
   over, around and through you.

When your body goes into deep relaxation, your mind should stay alert. Try not to fall asleep. If you do, the process is less effective.

After the ten or fifteen minutes has elapsed, redirect your attention to your breathing. You will notice it has become slower and intensely calm. Return your breathing to normal. Then sit up refreshed, invigorated and relaxed.

The centering method described above is based on a yoga relaxation technique known as yogic sleep. Further study of yoga can help you to perfect this method. Meditation, which is taught at east-west centers throughout the country, leads to a similar state of revitalization and calm. Benny Goodman, the clarinetist, meditated regularly before going onstage. Other performers chant mantras in order to center themselves. When you are centered you are lost in the present. All such practices tend to establish deep regular breathing patterns, soothe the nervous system, relax the body and refresh the spirit.

CHAPTER 9
GENERAL BREATHING EXERCISES

And the Lord God formed man of the dust of the
ground, and breathed into his nostrils the breath
of life; and man became a living thing.
                              - Genesis, Ch. 2, v.y.

Breathing

When Philip Smith broke his foot while running he
was utterly desolated. The injury, he conjectured,
would mean complete inactivity for months. "About all
I could do," he writes in his book, Total Breathing,
"were some breathing exercises learned during earlier
yoga and martial arts training." As the breathing
eased his pain, Smith became fascinated with its
mysterious, curative effects. Delving deeply into the
theory and practice of respiration, he discovered that
breathing was of enormous help in a wide range of
activities -- acting, singing, sports, meditation.
"Breathing, he concluded, is the "missing connection
for the integration and control of body and mind."

As we've already seen, yogic practice identifies
breath, prana, with energy -- with the life force
itself. Deep, even breathing practice at times of

stress puts you back in touch with an inner source of
energy. Deep breathing slows the heart rate and
neutralizes, at least for the moment, whatever stimulus
is making you panic. When the mind is fastened to the
primal rhythm of breathing it tends to become absorbed
and calm. Worrisome thoughts about the future recede.
One becomes completely subsumed in the present moment,
returning, in a sense, to the security and certainty of
the unborn child anchored safely within its mother's
womb.

Many performers, speakers, lawyers and instructors
utilize deep breathing techniques to stay physically
relaxed as well as to keep their energy flowing smooth
and continuously so as to stay on top of the situation
and avoid panic.

"Believe me, the key to relaxing during a
tournament lies in your breathing," writes tennis pro
Vic Braden. "If you don't breathe properly, your
muscles get tight and your strokes will be forced. All
the work that you've done on your stamina will be for
naught. If you think about the breathing process, your
muscles will relax. According to Michael Kiefer in his
article "Ins and Outs of Breathing", if anxiety is
fear of losing control and breathing is an involuntary
override, then perhaps consciously taking control of
breathing brings a sense of overall control.[1]

For a speaker or a singer, shallow uncontrolled
breathing is an invitation to disaster. First notes
and lines come out cracked and weak. Panic skyrockets.
Control is lost. Breathe deeply and evenly at the
beginning of a performance and those first notes will

---

[1]Michael Kiefer, Esquire, February, 1986.

be beautiful and full-bodied from that moment on, and you're off to a great start.

The exercises which follow will help strengthen your respiratory apparatus and make controlled, even breathing a habit rather than something to be struggled for in moments of stress. Commit yourself to practicing them daily, for breath control is a skill, and like any other skill can only develop over time!

> "She took a deep breath. The most dependable antidote for nervousness."[2]

Breathing

Deep Breathing Exercises

Most people use only the top portion of their lungs when they breathe without filling the bottom part. To breathe correctly, you must use the bottom of the lungs as well as the top, exactly the way you do while asleep. The following exercise concentrates on achieving deep regular breathing. It may be practiced at almost any time throughout the day. Ideally perform it (a) sitting cross-legged with hand on knees, palms facing up, or (b) lying flat on your back, arms by your sides, legs slightly apart.

1. Slowly draw a deep breath through the nose. Imagine the air that you are breathing is fogged and visualize it passing through your nose and throat into your lower abdomen. Do not raise your shoulders as you breathe in. Instead, let your lower abdomen expand; then

---

[2]Joseph Maclis, Magda V (a best selling novel based on a singer's life)

your rib cage. Try to expand the rib cage as
much as possible. In fact, feel an expansion
across the breadth of the rib cage and pelvis
so that if you place the palms of your hands
against the sides of your body, you feel them
being pressed apart. Let the back swell as
well. Think of "deep" as a place not a size.
You want to fill the depths of you with
prana -- breath, vitality, energy, strength of
life -- as you inhale.

2. Hold your breath for approximately 5 seconds.

3. Exhale slowly through the mouth until your
   lungs are completely empty. Then pause before
   beginning to inhale. As you exhale, feel the
   front wall of your abdomen and rib cage drawing
   up and in to meet the wall of your spine. Once
   again do not force this movement (don't pull
   in). Simply allow it to happen. The air
   passing through your teeth should make a soft
   hissing sound. As you exhale, say the word
   "relax" to yourself and allow your tensions to
   flow out on the outgoing breath. With each
   exhalation let yourself go a bit more.

4. Experience the thrill of a deeper and deeper
   release. Repeat at least 5 times.

   Continue to breathe in and out, but now begin
   to direct your breath toward specific areas of
   tension: neck, shoulders, jaw, forehead.
   Breathe into these areas and breathe out
   through them.

Note: As your respiratory system strengthens with time, the length of your inhalations and exhalations should increase. For example, you may begin by inhaling and exhaling to a count of 10 each, then progress to 15, 20 and finally 25.

Upper Body Breathing

1. Take a slow, steady breath through the nostrils. This time, fill the chest as much as possible, but take care not to push out the abdomen. Instead, the entire abdominal area should be pulled back toward the spine.

2. Hold the breath for a second or two.

3. Exhale slowly, deeply and steadily through your mouth until the lungs are completely empty.

4. Repeat at least 5 times.

Note: You may want to keep the palms of your hands placed against your abdomen so you can feel it rise and fall as you breathe.

These last two exercises can be performed sitting, standing or lying down. They will further strengthen your respiratory apparatus and give you getter breath control, as will the following 3-Part Breathing Exercise.

Three Part Breathing:

1. Sit cross legged, hands on knees, palms up, face forward, jaw relaxed. Make sure your back is straight, shoulders relaxed, abdomen pulled back to meet the spine. Feel an invisible line perpendicular to the floor passing through the spine, lengthening through the back of your neck and continuing on out the top of your skull, pulling you up toward the heavens.

2. Inhale deeply, slowly and evenly through your nose. Think of your body as a teacup into which air is being poured. (The bottom third of the cup is your abdomen, the middle your lower chest, the top your upper chest). Inhale first into the abdomen. Feel it expand outward and your lower back swell out as well. Next, feel your breath fill out the lower chest, pressing the rib cage apart. Finally, feel your upper chest fill out with air as the shoulder blades separate and your breast bone widens (shoulders remain relaxed).

3. Once your body is filled to the brim with air, hold your breath for about 5 seconds.

4. Exhale slowly and steadily through the nose, emptying first the upper chest, then the lower chest and finally the abdomen. When all the air has drained out of your body and the "cup" is dry, wait a moment, then begin to inhale again.

5. Repeat at least 5 times.

Calming Breath:

The following practice will fill you with a surprising sense of inner calm.

1. Place your right thumb against your right nostril, pressing it closed.

2. Close your eyes and slowly inhale, consciously directing the air toward the forehead. Imagine that the air you are breathing is tinted with a calming hue -- blue, pale yellow or green. Let the color fill your body, bringing relaxation, strength and harmony to all parts of your being. Imagine that tensions and unnecessary thoughts are being uprooted and set flowing toward your forehead, drawn along by your inhalation so that they can be expelled when you exhale.

3. At the end of the inhalation, clamp the left nostril shut with the fourth and fifth fingers of the right hand. Hold your breath for 10 counts.

4. Keeping the left nostril closed, release the thumb, freeing your right nostril. Exhale slowly and steadily. This exhalation will draw out the tensions and toxins accumulated during inhalation.

5. Repeat the entire breath, but reverse the procedure, keeping your left nostril clamped shut during inhalation this time, then closing your right nostril on the exhalation by covering it once more with your right thumb and releasing your left nostril.

6. Repeat for a total of 10 complete breaths, 5 on each side.

Shining Breath

This practice strengthens the abdominal muscles used in respiration and leaves you with a tingling, yet relaxed, "shining" sensation.

1. Inhale deeply through your nose to the count of 5.
2. With your right hand resting gently on your abdomen, exhale 20 times through your nose in short, sharp "panting" exhalations. Each time you exhale, pull the abdomen sharply back to meet the spine, then release it so you can pull it sharply back with the next exhalation.
3. Repeat 4 times.

Integrate your breathing exercises into your daily relaxation practice as a whole. I suggest the sequence outlined below for maximum effectiveness, though once again, go with whatever works best for you!

* 3-Part Breathing
* Deep Breathing, Upper and Lower Body Breathing
* Stretching Exercises
* Centering
* Shining Breath, Calming Breath

CHAPTER 10

INCORPORATING RELAXATION PRACTICE INTO THE
PERFORMANCE SITUATION

On the day of your lecture, performance, club, or business meeting, you should set aside enough time to go through the entire practice once without rushing -- the morning before an afternoon appearance, or in the early afternoon if you're appearing in the evening. Then, as the fateful hour approaches, whenever you feel yourself tightening up and your heart begins to pound a bit, close your eyes and take several breaths, holding each for a count of 5 and saying the word "relax" as you exhale. This is a bona fide behavioral control: in comes the energy, out goes the stress.

Next, if time permits, release whatever local tensions you feel accumulating with a few head rolls, shoulder rotations, drop-downs -- nothing major, just enough to recenter yourself physically. And use what you have learned about centering to clear your mind. You do not have to go through the entire procedure -- simply use the mind control techniques you've acquired to free your thoughts and visualize a wave of relaxation moving up your body. (Note: As you breathe, stretch and center here, concentrate on your breathing. This will help to clear your mind of encroaching anxiety. The exercises should be so familiar by now that you don't need to think about procedure at all!).

Now your mind is clear, your body relaxed, anxiety drained away. This is a good time to focus and psych up -- to fill your mind with positive images about your upcoming performance (see chapter on creative visualization). The final thing you should do before preparing to go on stage is drain yourself of excess tension, clear your mind and then refill it with positive thoughts.

Later, as the curtain rises, step up briskly to the stage or platform and take a deep breath. In fact, begin breathing deeply 30 seconds before you even face the audience. In addition to all the calming effects this kind of breathing induces, it will exhilarate and energize you. According to Dale Carnegie, the increased supply of oxygen will buoy you up and give you courage. Certainly, it is that through deep breathing you will discover not only relaxation but spiritual strength as well.

When your heart begins to melt into your stomach and your knees start to give way underneath and you can't open your mouth because your jaw is locked tightly shut with terror, it's all very easy for complacent souls to whisper "relax!" into your ear. They never tell you how!

What I've tried to do is exactly that: to tell you how, step by step. Concretely. Specifically. Precisely. It's up to you to master techniques as your own. When you take up this task, remember that starting anything requires a hard self-push to set things in motion until skill is developed and techniques become second nature.   Don't try to force results at first.   Half the fun is experimenting until you have discovered your own custom-tailored way. Remember, the key to success is not "will" power but "want" power.

PART IV

OTHER METHODS

In the next three chapters are additional methods
for dealing with fear and with the debilitating effects
of stage fright. These methods are more specific to
the problem than the previous ones. They are also apt
to be more costly, since they involve outside help.
But for those who prefer these, or have had
insufficient success with the previous methods, I
suggest considering hypnosis, biofeedback or the
Alexander method. There are, in fact, concepts and
techniques common to all of these methods, including
creative visualization and the following methods. It
is simply a matter of finding the most appropriate and
effective approach for yourself.

CHAPTER 11

HYPNOSIS IS HELPFUL

"During hypnosis I feel a surge of confidence, as though I had been authorized by myself to create."
   -Thomas Morgan, author, <u>The Power of the Trance</u>

"Creative ideas seem to flow into my consciousness when I am resting in a self-hypnotic or trancelike state, or in a contemplative mood."
   -Leonard Bernstein, composer-conductor.

Hypnosis is a method for creating an altered state of consciousness. These states occur spontaneously among those who concentrate intensely, perhaps while being absorbed in a performance or piece of recorded music. Often we need a moment to re-orient ourselves after these states. It is this intensity that hypnosis can recreate.

Although hypnosis has been both a parlor game and a vaudeville attraction, it does not create an enslaving Svengali-Trilby relationship. Currently, it is an accepted medical-psychological treatment, and a valid tool for coping with stress. Hypnosis is not therapy. It is a supersaturated level of concentration which can be used to enhance other forms of therapy. Also, hypnosis is a hyper-consciousness -- a narrowed inner concentration that helps create a sense of mastery over the body.

Hypnosis is not sleep, although the confusion dates back to the modern recognition of the technique. Dr. James Braid, a 19th Century Scottish surgeon, coined the term from the Greek word hypnos, which means to induce sleep. Although your eyes are closed at the outset, you are breathing quietly, and there is some alteration in consciousness when in a trance, you are not asleep. In fact, you become more alert in the trance state and enter a state of intense concentration. The mind is focused on potent mental images, those images which can help you overcome anxiety. You are then not "spaced out," but you are wide awake, focused within yourself. In the trance state, you alone are in charge.

There is simply no evidence to support the idea that hypnosis is dangerous. You are not controlled or manipulated. Hypnosis is not something a hypnotist does to you -- you do it to yourself. All that any hypnotist can do is tap your natural capacity for focusing, concentrating, imagining, visualizing, distancing, and blocking out distractions.

A hypnotist need not be charismatic, bewitching or spell binding. No black magic or sorcery is involved, and no flashes of lightning flow from any hypnotist's fingertips. The great paradox about hypnosis is that what appears to be a loss of control is an exercise in greater control. You must be willing to enter the trance state -- a shifting of psychic gears to reach a higher plane.

According to Herbert Spiegel, M.D., a highly respected hypnotist at Columbia University, only 25 to 30 percent of the population is not hypnotizeable.

Everyone else has some level of, in Spiegel's words, "trance talent," from the unimaginative and analytical Apollonians to the creative and intuitive Dionysians.[1]

In practice, hypnosis is related to two familiar functions: imagination and self-suggestion. The goal of hypnosis is to encourage these naturally-occuring abilities by using our inner forces to influence our consciousness. Because of its recognized value in relieving the nervousness and tension associated with speaking, singing, or acting in public, hypnosis is a wonderful tool for treating stage fright and resulting anxiety.

Consider the case of a 31 year old musician whose anxiety about a pending concert induced a tremor in her hands which rendered her incapable of playing.[2] The tremor first appeared when she noticed the player next to her was trembling and extremely tense. After only one session with a psychiatrist who taught her a self-hypnosis technique, she was able to imagine her pending concert performance and the trembling fellow musician by her side, while simultaneously maintaining a state of relaxation and comfort. She was then able to pursue a successful career as a musician, using her learned self-hypnotic skills to overcome performance anxiety.

---

[1]In Greek mythology, Apollo was the god of light, order, and reason; Dionysius, on the other hand, was the god of wine, excess, fantasy and fertility.

[2]Reported by Dr. Fred Frankel in the International Journal of Clinical and Experimental Hypnosis, "The Use of Hypnosis in Crisis Intervention, " 1974, vol. 22, pp. 188-200.

During hypnosis, suggestions aimed at enabling you to pinpont and achieve your goal penetrate the subconscious mind and remain active there, influencing your behavior. When you are in a trance, the hypnotist may suggest ways to deal with stage fright. He may tell you that based on past performance, you have no reason to feel inadequate or scared.

A student who is to speak in front of a class becomes increasingly nervous and freezes, causing a mental block. Encouraged by repeated positive suggestions through hypnosis, this block can be removed. The distraught student may say, "Yes, I am nervous, but I will use my nervousness in a constructive way." Under pressure one needs the serenity that hypnosis offers.

The subject must learn to cope with his anxiety by separating himself from it. Prior to speaking in class, and on a regular basis, one should try to become as relaxed as possible. To do this, take a few deep breaths (breathing slowly and easily through imaginary holes in the feet - an amazingly effective image), feel the muscles loosen, and, if possible, sense oneself floating. Then, with eyes closed, suspend all judgment and picture success on an imaginary split screen, one side showing the crisis situation, the other showing how well it was handled. Through the use of heightened imagery, one identifies the problem and faces it, but still distancing the self so that it can be handled successfully.

To be effective, be as concrete in your imagination as possible. By having something to do you can feel your mind, unblock the block, and reduce anxiety. All this can be done in a few minutes.

According to Dr. Erika Fromm, a President of the American Board of Psychological Hypnosis, an image that is particularly useful for treating anxiety is that of the patient's hand grasping an audio volume knob. "I show them that when they turn the knob clockwise, it heightens their anxiety," explains Dr. Fromm. "Just as they can do that, they can also turn the knob counterclockwise and reduce their anxiety. The knob is in the patient's hand, which is a symbolic way of expressing that he is in control and that he doesn't need to be controlled by his emotions."

Harvey Misel, hypnotist for many major league baseball players, often helps them overcome batting slumps by talking to them, relaxing them, and then injecting their minds with "uncut ego food." These images have more emotional impact on players who are in the relaxed state than those in waking states. Misel tells the athletes, "You are going to hit the ball harder." His players use a post-hypnotic suggestion by tapping the bat on home plate as a reminder to relax and concentrate, telling themselves, "To the degree that I want to fulfill my potential, I will play a winning, triumphant game."

Self-Hypnosis

According to Dr. Moshe Torem, M.D., "All hypnosis is really self-hypnosis." By this he means, of course, that all that the hypnotist does is to suggest, to guide or to channel. The goal of self-hypnosis is to make the hypnotist unnecessary as quickly as possible.

In self-hypnosis, very powerful mental forces, those of the unconscious, are put to work, and you can "program" your own subconscious mind. When the mental censor is off guard, you can suggest to yourself most of the images you wish to emerge in consciousness from the subconsciousness. It sounds forbidding, but is in fact rather simple.

Auto-suggestion should always be made in positive terms. In this state, you are receptive to suggestions on how to overcome anxiety and stage fright. A fringe benefit is the ripple effect: As you overcome one troubling symptom, you are better able to handle other aspects of your life.

Although there are a number of methods available, the following one, taught to me by Dr. Herbert Spiegel of Columbia University, is most appropriate. I discussed the problem of stage fright with Dr. Spiegel and this is what he showed me. The following exercises, like any, require repetition and patience.

One, look up toward your eyebrows, all the way up. Two, close your eyelids and take a deep breath. Three, exhale, let your eyes relax and your body float.

As you feel yourself floating, permit one hand or the other to feel like a bouyant balloon and allow it to float upward. As it does, your elbow will bend and your forearm will float into an upright position. Sometimes, you may get the feeling of a magnetic pull on your hand as it goes up. When your hand reaches this upright position it becomes a signal for you to enter into a state of meditation and increase receptivity.

As you reach this state, concentrate on the feeling of floating, and concentrate on a specific image. Some suggest using images of serenity or favorite places. Dr. Spiegel advocates using the

following form of image;   you then fill in your own
specifics:

    float with

                     split screen   creative
                                                body
worries   general
                                          audience

To actually do the exercise, use a three count, and perform the exercise sitting or lying down. At the count of one, look up toward your eyebrows; at two, close your eyelids and take a deep breath; at three, exhale, let your eyes relax and let your body float. As you feel yourself floating, permit one hand to feel like a bouyant balloon and let it float upward. At this point, enter a state of meditation and concentrate on the primary strategy. To bring yourself out of this state of concentration, count backward in the same manner: three, two, one. At three, get ready. Two, with your eyelids closed, roll up your eyes (do it now). And one, let your eyelids open slowly. Then, when your eyes are back in focus, slowly make a fist with the hand that is up and, as you open the fist slowly, your usual sensation and control returns. Let your hand float downward. This is the end of the exercise.

Now, I propose that in the beginning you do these exercises as often as ten times a day, preferably every one to two hours. At first, the exercise takes about a minute, but as you become more expert at it, you can do it in even less time. By doing this ten times a day, you can float into this state of bouyant repose; give yourself this island of time. When you are accomplished, you will have twenty seconds, ten times a day, in which to use this extra state of receptivity, to re-imprint these critical points.

In self-hypnosis you are, in effect, undoing the damages of years of fear. The unlearning may take time, but remember that to reach the state of stage fright also took time, and was also a carefully learned response, even if it may seem to be your natural state. Patience here, as elsewhere, is the watchword.

CHAPTER 12
HOOKED ON BIOFEEDBACK

A famous public speaker's story, perhaps apocryphal, goes like this. A toastmaster, who had practiced an introduction for the visiting Governor of the Virgin Islands, spoke beautifully for several minutes about the islands and the accomplishments of the governor's administration. He then concluded the introduction with a flourish. "It's a great pleasure," he beamed, "to present the Virgin of Governor's Island."

We all make mistakes in front of audiences, and no method on earth can prevent us from being human, nor would I want such a method. But we can, by reducing superfluous tension, do two things. One, cut down on the number of mistakes, such as the one above, produced by nervousness. And two, by reducing distress, enable us to face with equanimity, those mistakes we do make. One of the better methods for doing so is through the use of biofeedback.

Biofeedback is based on the fact that emotions cause physical changes. A blush of embarrassment is just as obvious as one resulting from strenuous exercise. When you face a group of people or a new

lover, your heart thumps just as rapidly as during or
after a three-mile race. Yet in neither of those
examples has the body consciously produced those
emotions. Fainting, blushing, sweating, or racing
heartbeat can all be produced by our emotions. We say
that these functions are involuntary and automatic
because until recently no one has been able consciously
to slow up his or her heartbeat. Biofeedbackers teach
you to do that -- to control what was previously
thought uncontrollable.

Dr. Elmer Greene, founder of the Biofeedback and
Psycho-physiology Center of the Menninger Foundation,
defines biofeedback as "getting immediate, ongoing
information about one's own biological processes such
as heart behavior, temperature, blood pressure, muscle
tensions." It is an extra tool that permits more
information to flow between the mind and body, sending
back information about the smallest, normally
imperceptible behavioral changes as they occur. This
expanded information aids the patient in influencing
emotional change.

My purpose in writing this chapter is to
recommend the benefits of biofeedback to stage fright
sufferers. I underwent training sessions with Kenneth
Greenspan, M.D., at Columbia Presbyterian Medical
Center in New York, to learn for myself what this
modality does to help alleviate stress and stage
fright. Under his supervision I learned how to attain
a sense of greater calm before performing and to relax
myself in basic life situations as well.

At each session I was hooked up to several
electronic monitoring devices and was made aware of the
mind-body interaction. These devices meter bodily
tension and relaxation. Because learning to relax is a

skill and a crucial prerequisite to success, I was also given a relaxation tape.

The first side of the tape took me through active relaxation exercises which consisted of exaggerating muscle tension by clenching and unclenching different muscles and then releasing the physical tension in order to discern the difference between the tense state and relaxed state. The other side of the tape involved a passive relaxation technique. Both sides used Dr. Greenspan's process of "focused breathing" and muscle relaxation. I was instructed to practice the tape twice daily. After a tense day, or before a lecture or a performance, the tape enabled me to change gears and plug into "a more positive realm."

Biofeedback is successful in part because most people react in predictable ways to acute or chronic stressful situations. Specifically, we react with the fight or flight response, which we discussed in an earlier chapter. It is an involuntary response sharing a common etiology with stage fright that helps us deal with and adjust to stressful or dramatic events. It may also cause us to overreact to these same events.

For instance, when the mind senses a threat -- a large audience, an important interview, a school board meeting, a courtroom full of reporters -- the body prepares to deal with the challenging event, to stand and fight or flee the danger. This response to our emotional environment involves the sympathetic nervous system as well as the whole gamut of hormonal agents. Starting in the brain, the autonomic nervous system and hormones regulate our responses, keeping us tense and alert, or allowing us to relax. The fight or flight response and the relaxation response are innate and biological opposites. Biofeedback exercises the underused relaxation aspect. That is why the relaxation response and meditation offer a natural balance to counteract stress, one which can also reduce dependency on pills or alcohol, food or other substances.

Through the use of machines that monitor physiological changes in the body, you can learn to increase mastery over involuntary functions (heart rhythms, intestinal relaxation, sweaty palms and voice changes) that were once thought beyond our control. Biofeedback machines are like biological Geiger counters, detecting stress patterns everywhere in the body. The result of this knowledge is an increased ability on your part to achieve a relaxed state through physical and mental control.

Most of us are familiar with those lucky people who do not need instrumentation to relax, but many other people find the equipment very helpful, especially in the early stages of relaxation. The goal, of course, is to learn to improve and to focus on internal and external stimuli. Eventually those same psycho-physiological response patterns can be achieved without continued reliance upon the machines. Let's see how a visit to Dr. Greenspan's center works:

First comes an initial visit with a physician, who will tailor the program to your own needs. The usual biofeedback session is an hour long. During the first ten minutes you relax and then are attached to a machine that supplies immediate information about your body. The therapist stays with you throughout the session, and together you discover how to diminish stress.

During this session the machines measure the changes in physiological activity and tell you whenever a tiny change occurs in the desired direction. Instant biofeedback expedites the learning process. The goal is to learn to lower muscle tension or blood pressure or increase hand temperature wherever and whenever necessary -- in the classroom, on stage, in the home or office.

There are many ways to receive information from the machines. It can be visual feedback conveyed by lights that you watch, or it may be sound feedback. A low-pitched tone indicates when the muscle is relatively relaxed, a higher pitch when the muscle is tense. You begin to associate the muscle's state to the feedback from the apparatus, and you learn to relax the muscles to keep the feedback at a low level. The critical point is that you can get immediate information about your own body.

At the end of the session you discuss and evaluate your progress with your physician.

To learn to stay calm and tolerate a healthier landscape for myself before a performance, I was connected to a machine whose electrodes were placed on my fingers and forehead. The machine is non-invasive (there are no needles); I felt no sensation whatsoever. Some such machines are battery operated and portable, as small as a pack of cigarettes, and they monitor body activities while you go about your daily routine.

No matter how simple or how complicated the machinery is, the best way to make it work is to visualize through imagery and auto-suggestion how the body will change. So I told myself what to do, I relaxed, and my body regulated itself. The instruments reflected the change. So you might say that the electromyograph, the EMG as it is popularly called, is an alternative approach to relaxation training. Since

I am a performer and nervousness belongs to performers, I benefited most from the deep relaxation training of the EMG machine. By quieting my mind and body, I conserved my energy and improved my concentration -- a must for a top-flight performance.

I heartily endorse biofeedback. It is guaranteed to help you succeed in overcoming stage fright. After just a few weeks of practice, you too may be capable of achieving the relaxation needed to convert stress into energy -- a relaxation you never dreamed possible.

CHAPTER 13

SAMPLING THE ALEXANDER TECHNIQUE

"Alexander established the beginning of a
far-reaching science of the apparently involuntary
movements we call reflexes."
-George Bernard Shaw, London Music

"The Alexander Technique opened me up physically
and tapped a resource in me that was tremendously
beneficial later in creating characters."
-Soprano Johanna Meier, Opera News, July 1982

Clarence Darrow, legal champion of the oppressed,
spoke with the whole force of his body as naturally and
skillfully as the matador engages his bull. Such
energy misapplied by a hair-breadth would mean tension,
fatigue, or disaster. The great communicators who
perform at their peak in pressure situations display
this mastery of movement. When Fred Astaire danced or
when a fashion model glides down the runway, there is a
sense of ease. According to the creator of the
Alexander Technique, F.M. Alexander, this quality of
relaxation in action is not just the result of natural
talent, but can be learned.

Movement is related to our emotions and
encompasses basic psychophysical activity. The release
of physical tension is the first step toward releasing

mental tension. Therefore, if we succeed in easing our physical movement, we can also free our emotions. In Wilhelm Reich's concept of muscular armoring, "the release of armor is generally accompanied by a strong emotional release."

Through physical self-awareness the Alexander Technique loosens up the body and allows for this greater freedom. The body can be compared to a violin string which needs enough tension to make music but not to snap. The technique was based on F.M. Alexander's personal need. An Australian Shakespearean actor, (1869-1955) Alexander suffered from a periodic loss of voice, a serious problem for any actor. At the turn of the century there was no available treatment except for voice rest, which helped only temporarily. All traditional medical treatment failed. Only with the aid of a three-way mirror did he discover that his loss of voice was due to the way he "used" himself. More particularly it was related to a "backward downward pressing of the head." He experienced a pressure at the base of the skull right before speaking. By creating this pressure he was interfering with his best coordination. He found that the least tendency to hoarseness was associated with a "lengthening of the stature rather than a stiffening." He functioned best when his stature lengthened, and this came about when he allowed a "use of his head" that he describes as forward and up in relation to his neck and torso. He cured himself, and was able to return to the stage, but chose instead to share his technique with those who faced the same problem. His personal students included such luminaries as George Bernard Shaw, Aldous Huxley and John Dewey.

For most of us, appearing in public is stressful. The more details of our daily life we can handle effortlessly, the more our concentration and energy will be available when needed to face an audience of even one person. Speech and breathing are movements as well and they function most efficiently when we are relaxed. Alexander's theory of primary control holds that tension in any part of the body is reflected in the head and neck muscles. Similarly, any excessive tension in the head and neck muscles resonates throughout the body -- everything is connected to everything else.

In order to experience personally this technique, I was recommended to Pearl Ausubel, a certified Alexander teacher. Workshops and group lessons of 40 minutes duration are available at universities and specialized schools such as Juilliard in New York or Guild Hall in London, but I preferred the special one-on-one teacher-pupil relationship.

Pearl explained that our balance is automatic when we are young, but over the years most of us misuse our bodies; all that is needed is to unlearn these habits. "Prevent the things you have been doing and you are half way home."

We can do this by delaying our habitual response so that a different response can occur. Through the gentle hands-on method, Pearl guided me through the mechanics of everyday physical movements. Astonishingly, some ways of using the body are better than others. I learned how to bend, kneel, sit, walk and stand all over again. Standing up is one of the simplest things we do every day, but it is the "most larded with excessive effort. There is so much gathering of force, so much getting set with the entire

body one might think we are off to the Augean stables,"
states Denise McCluggage in her book <u>The Centered</u>
<u>Skier</u>.

In one revealing flash, I discovered that I had
more energy when I suspended judgment, stopped thinking
of the end result (endgaining as Alexander called it)
by staying in the moment. So I let Pearl initiate
these basic physical movements. My thoughts steered
movements in the right direction. As close to me as my
shadow, she would actually move and adjust my knees,
arms, head and neck in the desired direction. On a
massage table, she had me visualize my head floating
like a helium balloon and the back smiling. Again the
hardest thing was the non-doing to allow Pearl's hands
to guide the movement. Unlike hypnosis: you keep your
eyes open -- that's the Alexandrian way.

Now what does this have to do with facing an
audience? Everything. When you walk onstage this way
you feel lighter and freer -- a spontaneous onrush of
effortless effort. With this "correct alignment" you
have more energy available for the challenge of the
situation. The image of floating induces a physical
relaxation, a feeling of being swept away beyond the
ordinary self. It is every creative person's goal to
float, to reach out and to soar. This is a proven and
effective way to attain that goal.

PART V

DRUGS: PERFORMANCE CATALYSTS

CHAPTER 14

DRUGS: A CURE OR A DETRIMENT?

Any kind of artificial device is bad for a
creative artist. Alcohol does not help you see
more clearly. Drugs do not help you see more
clearly. They make you <u>think</u> you see more
clearly, when, in fact, you don't see any clearer
than you do in dreams...No artist has ever created
better from being an addict of any sort.
                    -Ned Rorem, one of America's greatest
                    living song-composers and author of
                    many books on the art of performing.
                    (Ovation Magazine, October, 1983)

Can drugs provide a cure-all to the full spectrum
of performance ills ranging from stage fright to
creative impotence?   Or are drugs a dangerous crutch?
Is the drug-dependent performer a latter-day King Midas
who turns all he touches to gold?   Or is he rather the
Emperor-in-New-Clothes who parades around feeling like
a knockout ... and looking like a fool?

Certainly the practice of using drugs to induce a
creative, "inspired" state has an ancient pedigree.
Since time immemorial, primitive people have often
smoked or eaten mood-altering substances as a prelude
to ritual dances and ceremonies. In modern day India,
Kathakali dancers insert opium poppy seeds under their
eyelids several hours before going onstage.   Such

performers indulge these practices to experience _inner_ rapture as they dance -- to _feel_ inspired rather than to _be_ inspiring for an audience. Just because you feel more creative or inspired, though, doesn't mean you really are so at all! Drugs can't breathe talent into being where it does not already exist -- and there's every indication that almost all mood-altering substances actually impair one's capacity to deliver to an audience.

For years now, many top-notch performers have eyed mood-altering chemicals with keen suspicion. Drugs, they feel, befog the brain, retard the reflexes and take the edge off that precious, keyed-up "tingling" feeling so essential to an electric performance. "I don't take Valium or any of that crap," says dancer Ann Miller, "because it would dull everything."

Not everyone, however, is as disciplined as Miss Miller. Far too many performers, _particularly those who've experienced the misery of stage fright_, turn to pills or alcohol to escape from overwhelming feelings of terror and inadequacy. Whether downers to calm the nerves or uppers to build confidence, drug use in the entertainment industry has reached epidemic proportions.

This is hardly surprising as drug use has reached critical proprtions in American society at large -- in the world of business, politics, medicine and sports, as well as in the arts. We are a nation of externally-oriented people, obsessed with the notion that "commercial substances" can cure our every ill.

THE MEDICAL EVIDENCE (UNTIL A FEW YEARS AGO)
TRANQUILIZERS

Tranquilizers, the most widely prescribed of all

mood-altering substances, are potent anti-anxiety drugs. They cannot ultimately boost confidence, however, as they give only a false sense of security. In addition, they drastically impair physical capabilities and intellectual functions. Depressants can make you feel calm, but the sedative side-effects prevent you from meeting the performance challenge with a keen mental edge.

ALCOHOL

Mae West, famous for her wit and wisdom, once confessed, "My secret is positive thinking and no drinking."

Alcohol may provide a performer with a false sense of contentment, but it dulls the senses, numbs the brain, slows reaction time, interferes with coordination and dampens enthusiasm. In addition, as George Sheehan, marathon-running medical doctor, points out vis-a-vis athletes, beer, wine or hard liquor should never be used as muscle relaxants or as erbogenics (performance aids) because alcohol acts as a diuretic, causing water loss and so may lessen the heart's capacity to do its work.

MARIJUANA

Marijuana belongs to the family of hallucinogenic drugs and, as such, produces a disturbance to the consciousness. It has been claimed that marijuana increases creativity and enhances one's performance capabilities in other ways as well. Some of these claims have been objectively tested, especially in the area of musical performance. The results in this area have been uniformly negative.

There is evidence, moreover, that the consciousness-distorting effects of this drug make it difficult for a performer to accurately assess whether he's "on" or he's "off." In some cases, paranoia is induced. Several experts concur with Margaret O. Hyde, who said, "Excessive use of marijuana and the self-discipline necessary for creative productivity seldom go together."[1]

COCAINE

The "white lady" as cocaine has been nicknamed by users, is perhaps Hollywood's greatest _femme fatale_, and she gives her victims a feeling that they can do anything, a rush of enormous excitement and energy. While this may boost one's confidence and get one psyched-up for performing, the initial rush is frequently accompanied by the jitters and ends quickly, leaving one prey to an unmitigated and intense anxiety.

What's more, cocaine tends to impair concentration and blur one's connection with subject matter, fellow performers and the audience. Curiously too, while a coked-up speaker or performer may feel he's operating in high gear, his work sounds slow and unimpactful.

---

[1]Margaret O. Hyde, _Mind Drugs_, New York: Pocket Books, 1969.

CHAPTER 15
BETA-BLOCKERS: "NO GREAT SHAKES"
OR A CONFIDENCE PILL AT LAST

Am I then suggesting that drugs do not provide an answer to stage fright? Well, not exactly. Within our society, so pervasively medicated both benignly and malignantly, there may be a place for careful, controlled drug use in the treatment of performance anxiety.

Several investigators have recently begun to experiment with a class of drugs known as beta-blockers, most particularly with propanolol hydrochloride (propanolol for short) in order to test their effectiveness in combating stage fright.   The results have proven astounding.   Unlike alcohol and traditional tranquilizers,   such as Valium, beta-blockers calm without dulling. No drowsiness, no muddleheadedness -- all the heightened awareness to fine execution...even that precious tingling feeling all performers treasure -- yet no terror! Beta-blockers have been deemed the "confidence pill" which helps you "act like a winner and feel like one too."[1] Widely used by physicians to treat high blood pressure and heart problems such as angina, as well as migraine, beta-blockers suppress many of the somatic manifestations of anxiety, such as fast heart beat (tachycardia) and tremors. The drug works by interfering with adrenalin, a chemical secreted by the endocrine glands. Dispatched in times of danger, adrenalin prepares us for action by "alerting" or "activating" many, many adrenorecptors, minute cellular structures located in the nervous system throughout the body. The adrenalin hits/activates each receptor much as a multiple transmitted emergency telegram from the Pentagon would mobilize the many bases scattered across the United States. Each adrenoreceptor then has its own function in preparing us for action. Some of these, the beta-receptors, produce the following well-known symptoms of fear or stage fright: rapid pulse, pounding heart, trembling, sweaty palms, tight breathing, even nausea. (We should note that while all these physical changes may be quite useful for fighting or fleeing an enemy, they are extremely disruptive when you are trying to bow a cello or croon with a saxophone). Beta-blockers, then, happily lock into the beta-receptors and keep them from receiving adrenalin. Ergo -- no "danger" signal gets to the beta-receptors and so none of the above all-too-familiar symptoms are produced.

Yet how is it that beta-blockers can affect the nervous system itself, virtually inactivating certain neural receptors, and yet in no way affect one's perceptivity or level of alertness? The answer seems

---

[1]Anthony Liversidge, <u>New York Magazine</u>

to lie in the location of the beta-blocker's sphere of action. According to Dr. Brantigan, a pioneer in this research, its province is restricted to the peripheral (sympathetic) nervous system and does not spill over into the central nervous system, or CNS. Alcohol and tranquilizers do: alcohol by attacking the reflective and rational centers of the brain and by so doing reducing accuracy or thought; tranquilizers by slowing down the rate at which nerves transmit impulses to and from the brain, thereby decreasing both one's excitability and one's level of alertness. Both are termed CNS depressants, in fact. It's not too difficult to see the adverse effect such CNS depressants must have on performance values, whereas beta-blockers, leaving the CNS so entirely unaffected, preserve the performer's excitement, alertness and accuracy -- his ability to make subtle distinctions -- intact.

Our "confidence pill" was introduced to the entertainment world several years ago when a team of clinical pharmacologists from the Royal Free Hospital in London, headed by Dr. Ian James, hired Wigmore Concert Hall and engaged 24 string players, all with histories of stage fright, to perform under the influence of beta-blockers. According to an article in the prestigious medical journal, Lancet, performers all showed lower blood pressure, lower heart rates, steadier bowing. Beta-blockers are effective, however, only when the 'performer' describes his/her anxiety in terms of palpitations and tremors rather than in terms of psychic anxiety -- worry or mental tension.

Following quickly on Dr. James' heels, Dr. Charles Brantigan soon published similar results in the Rocky Mountain Journal. Dr. Brantigan, surgeon at the

University of Colorado Medical Center and part-time tuba player, together with his brother Tom, a teacher of the organ at the University of Nebraska, and Dr. Neil Joseph, ophthamologist, conducted a series of double-blind experiments in Nebraska and at The Juilliard School in New York. Students were asked to execute the exact same performance on two different occasions -- once with propanolol, and once without. According to reports in the Italian medical journal Senza Sordino, the drug drastically reduced the effects of stage fright without in the least impairing technical execution. In fact, teacher, performers, and critics involved noted significant improvement in musical accuracy, rhythmic stability and memory among propanolol users.

Encouraged by such results, enthusiasts speculate that propanolol could permit a performer who has become totally disabled by stage fright to return to the stage. They also suggest that the drug's use could be extended beyound the entertainment world to other high stress professionals -- airline pilots, trial lawyers, surgeons, executives, as well as to alcoholics and people who are afraid of flying.

As the Brantigans explain it, beta-blockers do more than simply relieve the physical manifestations of acute anxiety. They also affect the performer's mental state. For as we saw in the the chapter on Relaxation, stage fright has two components -- one mental and one physical; each feeds the other. When you start to shake and gasp for breath, panic skyrockets. How can you even begin to concentrate on the arduous task ahead, much less execute it with brilliance and aplomb when your hands won't stop shaking and you can't hear a thing except your pounding heart! With the increase in terror your physical symptoms increase. Beta-blockers eliminate this snowballing effect before it even begins. Because you are able to stay in physical control of yourself, you can maintain better mental control as well.

Researchers are quick to point out, however, that beta-blockade, though immediately helpful, is not a cure-all. Though beta-blockers improve performance, they do not increase the performer's ability; they simply free you to be yourself and play up to your ability at that moment. What is more, they only really work for performers who are more or less normal, healthy individuals with a normal level anxiety resonse to stress. When a person's stage fright is rooted in deeper neurosis -- low self-worth, over-dependence on the opinions of others to achieve self-respect, etc., they are only partially effective. Such a person won't be very reassured by finding himself in absolute control of physical reflexes, voice, hands, etc., any more than a beautiful woman who is convinced that she's unattractive will be reassured by seeing her face reflected in a mirror.

UNDESIRABLE PSYCHOLOGICAL AND BEHAVIORAL EFFECTS OF BETA-BLOCKERS

Beta-blockers are not completely benign drugs. They are strong stuff, and should never be given to people with asthma, hay fever, some strains of diabetes, or certain heart conditions. They should only be prescribed by a physician who is willing to oversee administration of the drug. Although, in comparison with the dosage level usually prescribed to high blood pressure or angina patients, doses given to counteract stage fright are terribly minute. Yet side effects are still possible. Potential mental side effects include fatigue, insomnia, depression, hallucinations, nightmares, and even sexual dysfunction.

Robert Temple of the U.S. Food and Drug administration is critical of the drug. "It would worry me considerably if propanolol were taken on the streets," he has said. Nevertheless, the FDA has since considered a proposal to improve the marketing of propanolol as a palliative for stage fright and other forms of anxiety; the proposal is now on hold.

IS DEPENDENCY POSSIBLE

A plus vis-a-vis propanolol, the most extensively marketed beta-blocker in the U.S. today, shows there seems to be little inducement for a patient to increase his dosage or to become dependent on the drug. "Small doses for musicians will do wonders, but doubling the dose will not make you perform miraculously!" says Brantigan. He adds: "Since there is no distinct feeling associated with the medication, many performers will find that their egos take over and start believing that it is their own super-human strength that's getting them through. They stop taking the pill and find they can perform well without it." In other words, if you believe you can get through the performance without a panic attack all on your own, you will!

As Dr. Conrad Schwartz, Department of Psychiatry, University of Iowa Hospital and Clinic, suggests: "Taking a pill deals only with the symptoms here, not with root causes." What if you discover, two hours before an out-of-town convention lecture that you left your propanolol at home? You're worse off than before you ever heard the word "propanolol" because now you could simply go into a panic over having left it at home! It's very dangerous to rely on anything other than your own inner strengths to get you through a performance. Overuse of propanolol or any other beta-blocker for that matter, can get in the way of your developing such strength. "It is meddling," said Dr. Schwartz.

The mark of a mature performing artist is not complete desensitization -- but rather the ability to control and master the surge of performance anxiety when it occurs. The techniques outlined in this book, if practiced, will provide you with ample means to do just this without chemical aid. And the advantage of these techniques is that they become part of you. You don't have to worry about misplacing them or being helpless. You will have the deep satisfaction of saying, after the final curtain has fallen, "I overcame."

Many, many artists, lecturers, and professional personages use beta-blockers regularly these days, though few will admit to this in public. However, according to a survey by Dr. Duncan Clark, a research psychiatrist at Stanford University, 22% of symphony and opera instrumental musicians in the U.S. are using beta-blockers for stage fright (Music Medicine, "Clinical Management of Performance Anxiety"). The wisest, however, do not depend on them in an absolute sense. They know other ways of overcoming stage fright. Beta-blockers simply make the task much easier and are often reserved for very special occasions such as performing a cello concerto with the Boston Symphony Orchestra or shooting a scene for a director who intimidates you terribly and has let you

know there will be only one take. Exercise caution!
Beta-blockers are simply too powerful to be squandered
on every public speech or job interview.

Our bodies try to help us through challenging
situations. When under stress our nervous system
produces its own chemicals -- endorphins --
sophisticated hormones or synthetic beta-blockers which
ease the anxieties of performing by modulating the
functions of our brain. Endorphins are hormone-like
substances produced by the body, similar to external
opiates which help the nervous system respond to pain.
Athletes, opera singers, dancers, normally produce
higher-than-average endorphin levels to cope with the
higher stress levels they face every day. External
opiates, tranquilizers, or even beta-blockers, disturb
the body's natural homeostatic mechanism.

UNFAIR ADVANTAGE
Is it cricket to take beta-blockers? Tom Hall, a
Chicago Symphony violinist, raises this question:
"Might not the use of potent prescription drugs by a
performer in an audition or an attorney in the
courtroom give an unfair advantage over the competition
just as it might to the athletes or racehorses?"

Performers continuously seek advantages in
competitions and auditions through all sorts of means:
special diet, vigorous training, outstanding coaches.
Proponents of the drug argue that if prohibition of
drugs is enforced, then all the means which enhance
performance should be banned as well. Fairness, they
suggest, might require equal access, but not
prohibition.

To some this is mere sophistry, to others the
argument seems valid. Whether or not you should be

using drugs is a question for which there is no simple answer. Each case is different. Your decision must rest, ultimately with you and your physician.

In assesssing your own particular situation, ask the following questions:

*Are there medical factors making beta-blockers hazardous to my health?

*How great is my need? Have I exhausted every other means available to me for dealing with this problem? If I were without the drug, would I know how to cope?

If you are already using it, ask yourself these questions:

*Am I overusing the drug? Am I taking it before situations I could probably get through without it, situations that don't really involve that much stress? In other words, am I turning it into a crutch?

*Are there any side effects, physical or mental?

*If the beta-blockers don't seem all that effective, are there any deeper causes of a psychological nature (such as fear of crowds or obsessive worrying) that are contributing to my stage fright? How can I work these through? I strongly believe that although beta-blockers reduce anxiety without slowing mental functions or physical dexterity, stage fright symptoms can be alleviated or worked through without drugs. This book endeavors to explore the means to attain this goal.

If you do decide to give beta-blockers a try, however, you are not alone. Reports one young intern at Johns Hopkins Hospital, "Many of us take a few milligrams before presenting our grand rounds -- to keep our knees from knocking. Stage fright comes in all shapes and colors."

PART VI

YOUR OWN PERSONAL SUCCESS FORMULA

CHAPTER 16

YOUR OWN PERSONAL SUCCESS FORMULA

> "Her secret? It is every artist's
> secret...passion. It is an open secret
> and perfectly safe."
>   -<u>The Song of the Lark</u>, Willa Cather

As Willa Cather explains, there is no hidden secret, no magic formula for performing well. Successful people work very hard to do what they love. Their aim is self expression.

No one should appear in public merely to show off, but rather to offer something. The raison d'être must be personal.

Success in public cannot be learned from the printed page alone, but by watching others and by personal trial and error. Success ultimately depends on our attitude; how much we love what we are doing. I hope this book inspires you to enter the world you thought existed for other people.

In an interview, Gloria Swanson once talked about one of her first performances as a young artist.

> "As curtain time approached, I was frozen
> with fright. I told the producer to keep the
> box office open so he could refund the money,
> since I was convinced that when I opened my

       mouth, not a single sound would come out...
       When the cue came, I sleep-walked onto the
       stage. I saw the lights, the other
       actors...heard the welcoming applause, and
       then I saw the sea of faces out front, and
       suddenly, unaccountably, I was totally calm.
       I thought: I have always been here, and this
       is where I belong. Every word came out
       clean, crisp and strong. It remains, even
       today, one of my most rewarding experiences
       of my life."[1]

This sense of belonging - of rightness on-stage - is everyone's dream. Some achieve it with greater ease than others. How quickly and painlessly it comes has nothing to do with talent. It results from relaxation and acceptance, with opening oneself up and releasing that self from the shackles of ego.

Ease evolves from both imagination and concentration. But most of all it has to do with a willingness to take risks, to fail if need be, to face the unknown.

In a sense, every performance involves the crossing of a threshold from known into unknown. No matter how much you prepare, you can never quite know what will happen once the "curtain rises." But if you can cross that threshold with the faith of a sleepwalker, as Ms. Swanson did, you just might find yourself "suddenly, unaccountably...and totally calm," thinking "I have always been here and this is where I belong."

---

[1] New York Times, June 13, 1982

PART VII

EPILOGUE: TALKING ABOUT STAGE FRIGHT

Four people in the limelight examine the issue of stage fright in their lives and how we can overcome it.

EPILOGUE

INTERVIEWS WITH FRANK CORSARO,
LAWRENCE J. HATTERER, M.D., BARBARA GORDON,
AND RAOUL FELDER

Frank Corsaro, internationally acclaimed opera
director, is best known in New York for his long career
with the New York City Opera which includes over thirty
productions. His sensational and controversial <u>Carmen</u>
was broadcast nationwide on "Live from Lincoln Center."
In 1984 he made his Metropolitan Opera Debut with
Handel's <u>Rinaldo</u>, and in 1982 his English debut at the
Glyndebourne Festival with Prokoviev's <u>A Love for Three
Oranges</u>.

Although his directing has taken him all over the
world, for many years he held acting classes for
singers and directors because, "It keeps you in touch
with the real problems that opera is all about." I
have had the great privilege of being a member of this
class. I must say the singers and directors were all
dedicated, ranging from the young aspiring performer to
the highly successful professional. They all
experienced stage fright - the fear will I be able to
do what I want to do? Aspiration always plays a part
in the stage fright phenomena - just as in life.

Shafer:

According to psychiatrists, we can't eliminate stress or stage fright from our lives, but we can learn to use it more productively, to allow the energy to convert into a good energy. From your experience, how does this happen?

Corsaro:

It begins the moment you admit the negative energy. What you're dealing with is essentially negative childhood memory. We call it a "tape loop", one played over and over again. The question for everyone is, am I good enough? When you see it for what it is, automatically that energy gets channeled into the aspiration part. By admitting it, you're defusing a negative thought and catching up to the reality of the fact that you are an adult now, you're here and about to perform.

Shafer:

So the only way to break the vicious cycle is to respect and admit fear and pay attention to it?

Corsaro:

A difficult first step. The tape loop usually contains a method of denying the importance of ourselves, one that was originally intended to prevent the losing of parental affection. That's what these old structures are about. All tape loops that tell you not to do something are essentially loops that are retained childhood love objects.

Shafer:

You have often described stage fright as "not being with yourself." How would someone, then, get with themselves."

Corsaro:

When we are onstage, actor, lawyer, teacher or anyone, we can think of the angles -- the audience reaction, our hair, the critics -- or we go for the center. For instance, an attorney has an emotional point of view of a case, probably fighting for justice. By touching off in himself a response to that concern for justice, he is automatically doing what a good actor does -- putting himself in the area of concern. So he's dealing with his aspirations.

Shafer:

Gertrude Lawrence said, "Attacks of nerves seem to grow worse with the passing years," but other performers believe that the cure for stage fright is experience, trusting yourself. How do you relate to this?

Corsaro:

It's simple: many people learn the wrong things with experience. They learn to lock off their tension and not really deal with it, so what they do is learn half-hearted measures to deal with their talent, and then use that as an indication of experience.

The other, more positive way is to be in touch with those areas of contrary response and to realize that one is feeding the other.

Shafer:

Actors, speakers, people who suffer from clammy hands and shaky knees employ a variety of self-help remedies. What do you think of beta-blockers (propanolol) for alleviating if not eliminating the symptoms?

Corsaro:

Like other such things, it's a temporary crutch. I'm not against things of that kind, but you cannot rely on them. By relying on these crutches you intensify the hold of the negative side and therefore it becomes more monstrous and you get more and more trapped into the childhood response. I would say drugs are certainly not anything you should rely on to carry you through a career.

Shafer:

In "Opera News" you said: "Whatever you are afraid to show will come out in your voice when you least expect it." Can you expand on that?

Corsaro:

Yes. In other words, if you are not in touch with the negative area of your response, and try to fight, overwhelm or block it out, that voice will be heard only as negative. And, despite every effort you make, it will demand attention. So, the more you give it attention by defusing it, the better chance you have of controlling it. Otherwise, it will control you, not only in terms of stage fright, but in creating patterns of response. By avoiding its appearance on stage and elsewhere, what you're really doing is propitiating it.

Shafer:

Mike Schmidt, third baseman for the Philadelphia Phillies, said that in order to reach his peak performance, he tries to keep his mind from thinking, and "to draw back and relax and enjoy myself and leave myself alone." How does the highly-trained, highly tense, highly schooled opera singer compare with the athlete?

Corsaro:

I think what Schmidt says in fact says it all. If he can do what he says, he's essentially accomplishing what any performing artist would like to do: eliminate all the negative influences and leave oneself alone.

Shafer:

Is that putting yourself on automatic pilot?

Corsaro:

That's a good way of putting it. It would mean that you're appearing to your best instincts and in a sense that's what dealing with stage fright actually is: converting all of the energies toward achieving what your best instincts would like you to accomplish.

Dr. Lawrence J. Hatterer is an Associated Clinical Professor of Psychiatry at the Cornell University Medical School and Associate Attending at the Payne Whitney Psychiatric Clinic of the New York Hospital where he served, taught and researched for over twenty-five years. He is the author of The Artist in Society: Problems and Treatment of the Creative Personality. Dr. Hatterer has produced and hosted programs for television and videotape and has appeared on many major network and local television and radio programs. In 1978 he established the Foundation for Education in Human Relations in order to better disseminate mental health information via television and video-cassette to the public. He and his wife, a psychiatrist, practice together and write a magazine column in New York.

Shafer:

Stage fright is a fear that presents no physical danger to our life. Why then is it so threatening?

Hatterer:

Stage fright is threatening because people often conceive of this experience as potentially damaging to their entire being, to their ego, to who and what they may be to the outside world and that can include everything from feeling a humiliation that occurred to them as a child or in some younger period of their life when they felt deflated in the presence of many people, to a literal sense of exposure of some element of their own nature they would not want exposed - a weakness, somebody in the closet in their own life. A sense that they are not adequate or are going to be revealed as a

137

human being that would be undesirable. So it can cover
a host of things - whether it's inadequacy or privacy
or exposure of their nature which they feel will
destroy their sense of worth as a human being.

Shafer:

There was an article in the New York Times on
6/17/87 about singer-songwriter Carly Simon - "Carly
Simon Triumphs over Her Own Panic." In this article
she confesses her terror in front of an audience:
"It's terribly paradoxical because I do enjoy doing it,
but when the anxiety comes on, the adrenalin is so
strong it topples me. I never know when it is going to
happen, except the larger the audience the more I feel
I've got to lose." Could someone like Carly Simon
benefit from the Zen masters' teachings? They advocate
facing fear squarely in the eye. By giving in to fear
can a person transform its energy?

Hatterer:

Another element of stage fright is the person's
experiencing physical, if not even discrete chemical
experiences which produce levels of fear that they may
not have been accustomed to dealing with. To have an
exposure of that sort that is physical discomfort and
fear of that discomfort and expressions of oneself
physically in the presence of small and ultimately
enormous groups of people, can be so damaging as to be
paralleled to the child being in a situation where they
feel they are so fearful that they may urinate or lose
some sense of control over their total physical being.
What can take place for some people is an in-touchness
with their own body and their own chemistries and
control over their chemistries to the extent that a Zen

experience or doing something transcendental or making
them sufficiently aware, not only of the dangers but of
the abilities to control one's own inner chemistries,
that it could conceivably be a therapeutic modality for
a situation such as stage fright in which one is
subjected to experiences that they have no control
over.

Shafer:

So, in other words, pushing through the fear may
be less frightening than living with the underlying
fear which comes from a feeling of helplessness?

Hatterer:

Yes, particularly where one's own bodily functions
seem to have taken over.   This is a book in which one
can understand how one's ego and one's body could
destroy one's ability to communicate to large groups of
people and the answers to ego problems and physical
endangerments that one experiences by the chemical
aspects are in this book.   It becomes the core of what
one needs to master and in fact the other core is to
use the endorphins, to use the energy level and the
excitement that comes from such an experience
positively instead of negative.   There are people who
get high once they get over the fear.   In fact, they
will often say on television that this program has no
energy. What they're saying is that the performers were
not high enough.

Shafer:

When it comes to success in public, mind and body
cannot be separated.   Our bodies are capable of
producing their own wonderful opiate-like substances to

meet dramatic events. Now drugs called beta-blockers are being widely used for the same purpose. From your experience, do these drugs suppress the body's natural ability to adapt positively to the stress response?

Hatterer:

They conceivably could, and this is why artists are fearful of tampering with their own mood states by taking mind altering substances including those that are certified by the FDA, and particularly those that are not certified but come from the street; they are significantly endangered. So it is quintessentially important that the emotional and intellectual balance that an artist has to have with using the inner energies, which may indeed be their endorphins or something else, which gives them not only the ability to transmit feeling and thought at a larger than life level but also to be innovative with it, because the artist-performer must take not only the content and the emotion and translate it as the author intended it, but often make it uniquely something else that they themselves bring to the part, and without that balance and that excitement, and the ability to be innovative with the emotion and the words and all the levels that are required, you have a person not only that has gone through a period of stage fright which dampens that, but remains deadened on the stage.

Shafer:

And also the root of a problem is not solved by taking a drug.

Hatterer:

The use of the drug in this instance is presumably going to protect the person from either the level of anxiety or panic or terror or whatever it is, all those emotions that freeze innovativeness or sometimes even memory, but it may be to solve all those other things we mentioned before, which is ego, self worth - issues that should not exist when a true pro goes on. All these other issues are not to be solved at that point.

Shafer:

What about the layman, the lawyer, the clergyman, the mother at a PTA meeting?

Hatterer:

For people whose entire lives are not on the line as professionals, I would have to go back to my original formulation, which is the fantasy or the belief very often that exposure of one sort or another - regardless of what that person's particular feelings of inadequacies relate to, sometimes it's fatness, sometimes it's stupidity, sometimes it's a sense of embarrassment for socio-economic reasons, - whatever their Achilles' heel is, is laid bare for more than one person to experience out there and make a massive assault on the ego. Those people with pathological stage fright have exaggerated notions of how they are going to be attacked by the audience in terms of these vulnerabilities. But you have to understand that they are idiosyncratic, they're unique. I've treated enough people who say they can't speak in front of people to know that they're unique, and they can be up to and including bizarre sexual guilts in their lives which they feel that somebody would know.

It covers an enormous spectrum but it always has to do with some fear of assault on the person's integrity, whether physical and/or emotional.

Author Barbara Gordon wrote an inspirational book filled with life and hope, a human drama to which every person can fully relate. Prior to the book, Gordon produced award winning documentaries earning an Emmy for herself. I'm Dancing As Fast As I Can became a box office sensation - a movie featuring Jill Clayburgh.

Shafer:

In your book, I'm Dancing As Fast As I Can, it is stated "the world is what it is, imperfect, a world of people - no heroes, no villains, just people. And you've got to learn to accept that, in yourself, and in the people you love." Pertaining to stage fright, must we also learn to accept and trust ourselves when facing an audience?

Gordon:

One is always nervous before a sea of strange faces, but the apprehension of stage fright vanishes once I begin to talk - once I get involved.

In therapy she learned to trust herself. She learned to trust her own strength.

Gordon:

Women especially are defined by other people. Don't be afraid to be yourself, both "on stage" and in real life. From my own experience I came to realize that people who display an inner strength are treated differently from those who don't.

Barbara Gordon lectures ten or twelve times a year, and is always shocked when people are interested in hearing her. "I don't have a big ego." But she did admit that after her lectures the question and answer period is always spirited and lively. She doesn't, however, think of imperfection as a factor when facing an audience, but rather advocates not to impose unrealistic demands on herself. "Once you know your limitations and realize you're not perfect, that nothing is perfect, you can go with the flow."

Along with other well-known personalities, Gordon contends, "You can feel when the audience is with you, and that makes the stage fright go away, and it makes appearing worthwhile." Truly reaching out toward other people, with a unique person to person communication, is the artist's reward.

Shafer:

As a writer, you are familiar with the mental and physical blockages that can severely reduce both artistic impulse and performance power. Since power of the imagination turns out to be one of our best assets, why then, if drugs dampen this power, do physicians recommend them and people take them.

Gordon:

The answer I suppose differs from person to person. Doctors can give surcease to pain. Pills can give surcease to pain. It may be worth the price for some people, even with the side effects. Everyone has to make an individual choice - with their physician. We are in an instant gratification culture. Some

144

people would rather be on pain killers than rebuild
their lives or solve their underlying problems. It is
such an individual choice. Many people with crippling
stage fright resort to alcohol and drugs, rather than
find their own inner solutions. Some people walk
around blocked and don't know it. Some people are in
an emotional coma. I am willing to endure bouts of
pain without medication - that's best for me. I want
to get rid of the symptoms - I want to face the demon.
It strengthens me every time.

Shafer:

I agree that pushing through my own fear is less
frightening than living with the underlying fear that
comes from a feeling of dependency and subsequently a
feeling of helplessness. Isn't this also how we must
face stage fright - squarely in the eye?

Gordon:

Every time you accomplish something on your own -
deliver a speech, take a plane trip without a crutch -
you get stronger. You build on success. You get
stronger every time you are flying solo. For so many
years I have depended on other things. It is quite
wonderful to just take a walk without pills. I feel
marvelously liberated.

Indeed, Barbara Gordon is flying high.

Raoul Lionel Felder is widely regarded as the nation's most expert matrimonial attorney. He has been profiled in a number of leading publications, print interviews, and has appeared on major talk shows across the country. Mr. Felder has been widely honored for his public service, and appreciated for his professional dedication.

Shafer:

Most people suffer terribly from having to face the public. On stage they are exposed to intense scrutiny and they fear they may act in a way that may humiliate them. You have a long successful career in the spotlight - a reputation as the premier matrimonial attorney. How do you prepare your clients, ordinary people in extraordinary circumstances, to face a courtroom full of strangers? What techniques and strategies do you find most effective?

Felder:

We don't really prepare the clients in terms of stage fright. What I try to do is, I explain to them what the courtroom is going to look like, who is going to be there, physical dimensions. People are overwhelmed by physical dimensions. So many times a courtroom is nothing more than an office. They are all disoriented when they think they will see something out of Perry Mason. Thus, I try to give them an idea of the physical set-up. Most important, I tell my clients that all of the spectators sitting in the courtroom don't care about them; nobody cares. Everybody is egocentric: involved in their own thing. Part of a

146

lawyer's problem is even to get a judge to really
concentrate on their position, let alone the people
sitting in the courtroom. This I guess is the exact
opposite of the person who has stage fright because
people are there watching them.

Shafer:
When I say stage fright I'm really referring to
appearing in public. It could be a toast master at a
wedding or it could be a woman at a PTA meeting. For
both there is a level of aspiration, a stress factor.
Especially in your profession where these clients are
facing a firing squad.

Felder:
Basically we go over and over the material.

Shafer:
Preparation.

Felder:
But you can't cross the line where they memorize,
that's bad. They fall apart if somebody breaks the
trend. I tell them to forget about how they look and
so forth, except for the first sentence, worry about
the context of what you are trying to say. Recently we
had a young lawyer argue a case involving a relatively
minor question in an appellate court, first appellate
case he ever argued, and he seemed to be having
trouble. I told him to forget about how he looks or
sounds, to concentrate on the context, and he said that
carried him through.

Shafer:

You mean you wanted him to focus in on the material on hand, the concerns of the case.

Felder:

Yes, the material at hand, what the problems are, NOT how you are going to look. That will take care of itself. The first sentence is usually the most important I find because that will carry you through. It is always the first few seconds. But in court I represent a lot of actors over the years. Actors and actresses have a bad time in court because it is their own lives on the line. I remember one lady who was a star of a well-received national television show. They used to have uncontested divorces in most states of the union, New York also, where you were asked four questions, and if the lawyers weren't too experienced the clerk would hand you a printed set of questions, and you would ask the client. It was programmed so that basically the client had to answer little more than yes or no, except for one question - "Explain what happened on this date." This lady was so upset that she sat holding my hand. I was distracted. I had four finger marks on my hand from her fingernails, and she was an experienced actress, who later on became very well known. That sort of stuff. Recently, as a sort of corollary to this, there was a television talk show host here and he saw that I had some photographs on the wall. He looked at my pictures, and I said, "Notice that you never see a person, or if it is a person it is so far away - taken with a telephoto lens, because I could never bring myself up to saying 'Do you mind if I take your photo?'" Now this producer of a television crew said to me, he has the same problem. When he takes photographs, he can't go over to people and say, "Do you mind if I take your photograph?" However, for his job there is no problem at all.

Shafer:

Because he is focused on and concerned about the work rather than himself.

Felder:

They do M.O.S., men on the street. They stop people on the street, strangers, and it is no problem at all. It's interesting.

Shafer:

Once the ego is involved.

Felder:

What other hints do we give people? Material, material, material. That's the thing, you have to master your material.

Shafer:

They say know your material backwards and forwards. But for God's sake, say it forward.

Felder:

Even now, after thirty-five years, before I go to court I play what I am going to say in my head before I go to court. I play with the thing in my mind, exactly what I am going to do. I play it, and replay it, and replay it.

Shafer:

It's very good that you said that. That's creative visualization.

Felder:

And I do it right before I go to sleep. You do it before you go to sleep and somehow it gets ingrained. I never memorize. That's a terrible mistake, to memorize. One experience I had was when I used to do a weekly spot for CNN. They had a teleprompter, but when I was there I found that I would read the paper until I virtually had it memorized. But still, I'd use the teleprompter so I wouldn't have to totally depend on the reading. The technique for the newscaster is that it seems that they are reading the paper, but they're not. Once one of the secretaries skipped a page in the typing, so at the very list minute they put it on the teleprompter. Thankfully, I remembered enough about the general concept of the subject matter to keep going until it picked up right.

Shafer:

So you kept the intelligibility.

Felder:

Now that was unusual because in television if you have a problem you have to be on the mark. But most of the time I will never memorize. What I do is this... Make an outline of the key points. Any day that I am in court I have an outline, and I go over those points and re-read and study them. If it's long, then I make a longer outline. As you know, it is better to reduce that outline until you can have it on a 3" x 5" card, the entire talk. I am a plodder. I like to plan. I don't like surprises, although recently I attended an affair with all the legislators in the New York area who supported the Gulf War. As I walked in, I was told that I would present the award to Congressman Gary Ackerman. I didn't know I was going to do this when I was invited, and I didn't know anything about the Congressman. So what I did was I listened to the other people talking, made inquiries, and utilized the "waiting" time.

Shafer:
  You were formulating your thoughts.

Felder:
  I was formulating my thoughts. Then I just went into it. It was very hard. Most people are like the politician with the standard speech. They have 14 or 15 pat speeches, and they maneuver the questions around that. Lawyers on an appeal may have 14 or 15 points, and when the court asks you questions you twist it around for one of those points. But memorizing is...

Shafer:
  ... is deadly.

Felder:
  Deadly because it is not alive. I can't emphasize enough that I never read an address. I've addressed all sorts of organizations, and I have never memorized.

Shafer:
  Whereas performers usually encounter accepting audiences, trial lawyers and the people they represent

are thrown into an adversarial situation - lion's den. How do you train your staff to allay the fears of your clients in the face of coldness, rejection, and hostility?

Felder:

I represented Robyn Givens in her divorce. A poll was taken and she was one of the most hated women in America, hated by 80% of the population. Her mother was hated by 100% of the population. This was both unfair and inaccurate. They were, in fact, sensitive and lovely people. At one point in the divorce I was on a television talk show, and the audience was extremely hostile. It was more like a lynch mob. I think all you can do in a situation like that is talk softer and softer because there's no point screaming at a lynch mob. They're not going to hear what you want them to hear. They have choreographed themselves emotionally to only hear what they want to hear. In the courtroom very often you will see that cloud go over the judge's eyes - he's made up his mind. So you learn to deal with it. It's not personal. What you do in court is just keep talking to make the record clear. What I do is if there is some little mistake that I've made, I seize upon that as an opportunity to admit that an error was made.

Shafer:

So, in other words, you admit that you are human.

Felder:

"We made a mistake in this case, Judge, and we are in error." Usually it is a little thing, but suddenly you may have the Judge saying, "Yes, you made a mistake, but it's not that big of an error." Now he is listening, and you have his attention again. I don't believe that jokes get anybody's attention. I think that there is a pecking order with jokes. For instance, a jury laughs at a judge's jokes, but not at the lawyer's. If the same joke is told by a guest, nobody laughs, but when the host tells it, especially if the guest is a professional comedian, they'll laugh at it more. All the same joke, said in the same way...Maybe I can explain it more clearly. Have you ever heard the phrase "tabula rasa"? It's a legal term meaning blank wall or clean slate. I think people project on this tabula rasa whatever they need, and then it comes back to them. Another strong factor is how you are introduced. If you get a a weak introduction you will be poorly received. Still, I've faced a number of hostile jurors. You have to watch body signals. As an example, believe it or not, people nod their heads when they are agreeing with you, and although it may sound primitive, if a jury comes in and they're not looking at you, you've lost the case. Whereas if they are looking you in the eye, you've probably won the case.

Shafer:
    So you are attuned to all of these subtleties.

Felder:
    You <u>have</u> to notice these things, not only in the courtroom, but in life situations as well. It's just like a woman. You can feel when she is responsive or falling for your lines. Communication is basically people falling for your line. You are making love to someone and all the time it is the same thing. Making

love is not just the last act...it's also convincing
and seducing. It seems to me that communication is 90%
seduction. You want that person to believe you. And
you want to make them believe that you really are
concerned. It's very important. We are talking about
different skills. One skill is addressing an audience.
You are convincing somebody, like a jury, and you want
them to believe that you are reasonable, that you're
not angry. Interesting if you watch those who make it.
You can turn off the television, turn off the sound,
and you will still understand what they are saying.

Shafer:

Everyone who speaks in public is a performer of
some sort. Could you describe your first experience as
a trial lawyer?

Felder:

First experience in terms of my first full trial?

Shafer:

The one that was the most impactful back in your
salad days.

Felder:

Well, shortly after I started practicing, within a
couple of years, I went into the government, and got
dumped on me a case load that was extremely complex.
It had to do with income tax fraud involving bogus
shipments to Casablanca. The judge that was assigned
to the case was the worst judge they ever had.
Everyone hated him. He was a stickler. So, I
inherited this case, but I thought to myself, this is a
wonderful experience.

Shafer:

So your attitude was good.

Felder:

I just thought, "This is a wonderful experience. What are they going to do, shoot me? I'll either be made or broken by this one case, and if the latter happens then I will leave the government." You basically have to have confidence and be prepared for that one throw of the dice, and it will make or break you. Otherwise life is not long enough to take these little itty bitty chances that can mentally improve your skills. Somewhere you are going to have to go out on that stage, and take a terrible chance.

Shafer:

You are going to have to go for it.

Felder:

If you have an opportunity to sing a role, and you say, "Well, I am not equipped for it," baloney. You do it, and if you fail it is not a capital crime. Because you may never get the chance again.

Shafer:

That's right. It's a confidence that you had in yourself and you knew you could do it, and you obviously did.

Felder:

Also, I always felt that I had the intelligence and the technical skill. I had the ability to master these hundred little details for law.

Shafer:

According to psychiatrists, we can't eliminate stress or stage fright from our lives, but we can learn to use it more productively, to allow the energy to convert into good energy. You obviously have found the winning formula. From your experience, how does it happen? Again, when I say stage fright I mean podium prowess.

Felder:

I'll tell you the truth. I don't get stage fright.

Shafer:

You don't feel the adrenalin surging?

Felder:

Yes, I feel the adrenalin surging, but it's not stress.

Shafer:

It's eu-stress; good stress as opposed to distress.

Felder:

I get anxious when they call cases - one, two, three, four. I hate that. I keep thinking I will miss the case. But once I stand up it doesn't bother me.

Shafer:

In other words, you have a keyed-upness, a high once you start. The noted physician, Hans Selye, says stress makes for a peak performance. We have to take that nervous energy and convert it into positive energy.

Felder:

That's true, unless it's a debate with a person I
don't like. Part of the trick to me is don't get
yourself personally involved. If someone is attacking
you, and you feel you have to answer, you lose. That's
when you go crazy and get anxious, and then you blow
it. You have to just smile, talk about the issue, and
don't get involved. I try not to be drawn into that.

Shafer:

Well, you certainly have a reputation for being
good at it.

For some, public speaking is as painful as dental
surgery with symptoms ranging from shaky hands, wobbly
knees, memory loss, accelerated heart rate, dry throat,
even vomiting. How do you direct clients, already
overwhelmed, to deliver their statements (under
cross-examination) as clearly and calmly as possible?

Felder:

Well, although this is a very important event in
their lives, you have to make your clients feel that
the world doesn't revolve around them. In other words,
make them feel comfortable. I joke with them. I say,
"You know what the judge is thinking?...about what he
is going to have for lunch." I say there ought to be a
sign outside of every courtroom that says WHO CARES.
Also, you can't go over the material too many times for
it shouldn't be too studied. Under certain
circumstances that might work. For instance, Winston
Churchill practiced speaking in front of a mirror, and
planned every step, but in the case of my clients,
people who are already overwhelmed and unaccustomed to

public speaking, I encourage them to come across as natural and simple as possible.

Shafer:

We are rarely so vulnerable as when we stand before an audience - in your profession, a judge and jury. Many people would rather risk bullets than be in this position. Could you describe how your shyest, your most aggressive, and your most intelligent clients fared when they found themselves on the stand?

Felder:

Contrary to what one would assume, an aggressive person does not do particularly well when the underpinnings are pulled out. Usually the well-adjusted person does the best. A shy person comes across a bit shy. So what? Then there's the person who wants to tell jokes. Well, as I said before, no one should tell jokes in public except the comedian. No one really needs it. Certain personality traits are self-defeating, such as when a client tells a joke or uses flowery language. The same goes for the lawyer. If they're speaking in a way that's not comfortable to themselves they sound like jerks.

Shafer:

In the end we must be true to ourselves.

Felder:

Yes, and if at all possible, tell people what they want to hear. Then they will listen, and think that you are wonderful. That is the secret of it all.

REFERENCES

1. Howard Goshorn............from How to Speak Like a
                              Pro, page 5.

2. Ronald Colman............."And you look out at the
                              audience -- a terrifying
                              monster with a thousand
                              heads." page 13.

3. Willa Cather.............."There are some things
                              you learn best in calm,
                              and some in storm. You
                              learn the delivery of a
                              part only before an
                              audience." page 13.

4. Mae West to
   Charlotte Chandler........"I heard the applause --
                              applause just for me --
                              and I knew they really
                              liked me. I've never been
                              more secure than when I'm
                              on stage." "It was my
                              first love affair with my
                              audience and it lasted
                              all my life."   page 13.

160

10. Arthur Rubinstein.........Obituary quote, <u>New York Times</u> page 18.

11. James Coco..............."Forget about the big black giant. I look upon the audience as just living breathing human beings. We get our vibes from them." page 18.

12. Ellis Rabb..............."It's chemistry, that's all we are working toward." page 18.

13. Alec McCowen..............is certain that if you assembled Sir Laurence Olivier, Sir John Gielgud and all the foremost actors of the world upon a stage, and a cat wandered onto the stage, the audience would watch the cat. Why? "Because they don't know what the cat is going to do. The cat is natural." page 19.

14. Kurt Russell..............page 19.

15. John Wolfe...............<u>You Can Speak in Public</u>, page 19.

16. Robert Frost.............."The people I want to hear about are the people who take risks." page 22.

17. Leontyne Price...........believes that giving the audience "an emotional experience is your reason at the moment for being alive." page 22.

18. Hans Selye...............<u>Stress Without Distress</u> page 26.

19. Chris Evert Lloyd........"I knew I was in trouble when I didn't feel anxious." page 27.

20. Dr. Victor Pease.........<u>Anxiety into Energy</u>, page 28.

21 Seymour Bernstein........."Moreover, the wondrous playing of such artists as Arthur Rubinstein and Gregor Piatigorsky derives more from their ability to channel their nervous energy than from the maneuvers they take to allay its effects." page 28.

22. Frank Corsaro............"Yes, but you threw away
the very thing that would
have helped you. You
must use your nervousness
to show us this
character. If you plan
what you will show us,
and repress everything
else, you become
conventional." page 29.

23. George Sheehan............How to Feel Great 24
Hours a Day page 31.

24. Dr. Norman Vincent Peale.."I have never stood in
the wings of an
auditorium or in a pulpit
in church without
offering a prayer in
which I send out love
thoughts to the people
in the audience or
congregation." page 31.

25. Flip Wilson..............."What you see is what you
get." page 35.

26. Ralph Waldo Emerson......."Imagination is the
health of every man."
page 35.

27. Joseph Campbell..........The Hero with a Thousand
Faces, page 35.

164

28. Charles Garfield..........<u>Peak Performance</u> page 36.

29. Lars-Eric Unestahl........"the winning feeling"
                              page 37.

30. Shakti Gawain............"a technique for using
                              your imagination to
                              create what you want in
                              life...fulfillment,
                              enjoyment...rewarding
                              work, self-expression,
                              health, beauty,
                              prosperity, inner peace
                              and harmony." page 38.

31. Bruce Jenner............."I have always felt my
                              greatest ability was not
                              my physical ability, it
                              was my mental ability."
                              page 39.

32. Arnold Schwarzenegger....."All I know is that the
                              first step is to create
                              the vision because when
                              you see the vision,
                              there, the beautiful
                              vision, <u>that</u> creates
                              the 'want' power.
                              My wanting to be
                              Mr. Universe came about
                              because I saw myself so
                              clearly being up there on
                              the stage and winning."
                              page 39.

33. Charles Siebert..........."much of the story occurs prior to the event -- they remain out of sight, honing their skills and concentration, and then emerging for one or two moments of the extreme execution during which their picture either coalesces or crumbles." page 40.

34. Jack Nicklaus.............Golf My Way, page 40.

35. Jessye Norman............."Singing takes place in the brain." page 41.

36. Stephen M. Kosslyn........Mental Imagery Ability from Human Abilities, page 42.

37. Eloise Ristead...........Soprano in Her Head, page 45.

38. Simone Weil..............Waiting for God, page 46.

39. Eva La Gallienne.........New York Times editorial regarding Eleanora Duse published a day after her death. page 56.

166

40. The King and I............Anna sings, "Whenever I
                              am afraid I hold my head
                              erect so no one will
                              suspect I'm afraid/The
                              result of this deception
                              is very strange to tell,
                              Whenever I fool the
                              people I fear I fool
                              myself as well." page 62.

41. Genesis, Ch, 2, v.y.......(Bible) page 77.

42. Philip Smith..............Total Breathing, page 77.

43. Vic Braden..............."Believe me, the key to
                              relaxing during a
                              tournament lies in your
                              breathing. If you don't
                              breathe properly, your
                              muscles get tight and
                              your strokes will be
                              forced. All the work
                              that you've done on your
                              stamina will be for
                              naught. If you think
                              about the breathing
                              process, your muscles
                              will relax. page 78.

44. Michael Kiefer..........."Ins and Outs of
                              Breathing" in Esquire,
                              Feb, 1986. page 78.

45. Joseph Maclis.............from <u>Magda V</u>: "She took
a deep breath. The most
dependable antidote
for nervousness."
page 79.

46. Thomas Morgan.............<u>The Power of the Trance</u>,
page 91.

47. Leonard Bernstein........."Creative ideas seem
to flow into my
consciousness when
I am resting in a self-
hypnotic or trancelike
state, or in a
contemplative mood."
page 91.

48. George Bernard Shaw.......<u>London Music</u>, page 105.

49. Soprano Johanna Meier....."The Alexander Technique
opened me up physically
and tapped a resource in
me that was tremendously
beneficial later in
creating characters."
<u>Opera News</u>, July, 1982.
page 105.

50. Denise McCluggage.........<u>The Centered Skier</u>,
page 108.

51. Ned Rorem................"Any kind of artificial
device is bad for a
creative artist. Alcohol
does not help you see
more clearly. Drugs do
not help you see more
clearly. They make you
think you see more
clearly, when, in fact,
you don't see any clearer
than you do in dreams...
No artist has ever
created better from being
an addict of any sort."
Ovation, Oct, 1983,
page 111.

52. Margaret O. Hyde..........Mind Drugs, page 114.

53. Anthony Liversidge........(Beta blockers have been
deemed the "confidence
pill" which helps you)
"act like a winner
and feel like one too."
New York Magazine,
page 116.

54. Lancet....................from Lancet medical
journal, page 117.

55. Dr. Brantigan.............from Rocky Mountain
Journal page 117.

56. Willa Cather..............from <u>The Song of the
Lark</u>: "Her secret? It is
every artist's secret...
passion. It is an open
secret and perfectly
safe." page 127.

57. Gloria Swanson............Interview with the <u>New
York Times</u> June 13, 1982,
page 127.

BIBLIOGRAPHY

BIBLIOGRAPHY

Books

Aaron, Stephen. _Stage Fright: Its Role In Acting_.
Chicago and London: The University of Chicago
Press, 1986.

Allen, Steve. _How to Make a Speech_. New York:
McGraw-Hill Book Company, 1986.

Arieti, Silvano. _Creativity: The Magic Synthesis_.
New York: Basic Books, 1976.

Bach, George and Torbet, Laura. _The Inner Enemy: How
to Fight Fair with Yourself_. New York: Berkley
Books, 1983.

Baker, Janet. _Full Circle_. New York: Julia MacRae,
Franklin Watts, Inc., 1982.

Basmajian, John V., ed. _Biofeedback: Principles and
Practices for Clinicians_. Baltimore and London:
Williams and Wilkins.

Baxter, Marty. _Overcome Stage Fright_. New York:
Bradley Publications, 1982.

Beece, H.R., Burns, L.E., and Sheffield, B.F.
_A Behavioral Approach to the Management of Stress:
A Practical Guide to Techniques_. New York:
John Wiley & Sons, 1982.

Benson, Herbert, M.D. with Klipper, Miriam Z.
The Relaxation Response. New York: Avon
Publishers, 1975.

Benson, Herbert, M.D. _The Mind Body Effect: A Trusted
Guide to the New Medicine_. New York: Simon and
Schuster, 1979.

Benson, Herbert, M.D. with Proctor, William. _Beyond
the Relaxation Response: How to Harness the
Healing Power of Your Personal Beliefs_. New York:
Berkley Books, 1984.

Benson, Herbert, M.D. with Proctor, William. <u>Your Maximum Mind</u>. New York: Avon Books, 1987.

Bernhardt, Dr. Roger and Martin, David. <u>Self-Mastery Through Self-Hypnosis</u>. Signet, New American Library, 1977.

Borysenko, Joan, Ph.D. with Rothstein, Larry. <u>Minding the Body, Mending the Mind</u>. Reading, Massachusetts: Addison-Wesley Publishing Co., Inc., 1987.

Buscaglia, Leo, Ph.D. <u>Personhood</u>. New York: Fawcett, 1978.

Campbell, Joseph. <u>The Hero with a Thousand Faces</u>. Princeton: Bolliger Series, 1949.

Carnegie, Dale. <u>Public Speaking</u>. New York: Pocket Books, 1956.

_____. <u>The Quick and Easy Way to Effective Speaking</u>. New York: Pocket Books, 1962.

_____. <u>How to Stop Worrying and Start Living</u>. New York: Pocket Books, 1984.

Chaikin, Joseph. <u>The Presence of the Actor</u>. Antheum, 1980.

Connery, Donald S. <u>The Inner Source: Exploring Hypnosis with Dr. Herbert Spiegel</u>. New York: Holt, Rinehart and Winston, 1982.

Cooper, Morton. <u>Change Your Voice, Change Your Life</u>. New York: Macmillan Publishing Co., 1984.

Cousins, Norman. <u>The Healing Heart: Antidotes to Panic and Helplessness</u>. New York and London: W.W. Norton & Co.

Desberg, Peter, Ph.D. and Marsh, George D., Ph.D. <u>Controlling Stagefright: Presenting Yourself to Audiences from One to One Thousand</u>. Dominguez Hills: California State University, 1988.

Dudley, Donald L. and Welke, Elton. <u>How to Survive Being Alive</u>. Garden City, New York: Doubleday & Company, Inc., 1977.

Dunkel, Stuart. The Audition Process: Anxiety
    Management and Coping Strategies. Stuyvesant,
    New York: Pendragon Press, 1989.

Dyer, Dr. Wayne W. The Sky's The Limit. New York:
    Simon and Schuster, 1980.

Epstein, Joseph. Ambition: The Secret Passion. New
    York: E.P. Dutton, 1981.

Fletcher, Leon. How to Speak Like a Pro. New York:
    Ballantine Books, 1983.

Fox, Allen. If I'm the Better Player, Why Can't I Win?
    A Psychology of Competition. New York: Simon and
    Schuster, 1979.

Freudenberger, Herbert, M.D. Burn Out: The High Cost
    of High Achievement. New York: Anchor Press,
    1980.

Funke, E.L. and Booth, J. Actors Talk About Acting.
    New York: Avon, Discus Books, 1961.

Gallwey, W. Timothy The Inner Game of Tennis. New
    York and London: Bantam Books, 1974.

Garfield, Charles A., Ph.D. with Bennett, Hal Zina.
    Peak Performance: Mental Training Techniques of
    the World's Greatest Athletes. Los Angeles:
    Jeremy P. Tarcher, Inc., 1984.

Gawain, Shakti. Creative Visualization. Toronto:
    Bantam Books, 1978.

_____. Meditation: Creative Visualizations
    and Meditation Exercises to Enrich Your Life.
    New World Library, 1991.

Gelb, Michael. Body Learning: An Introduction to the
    Alexander Technique. New York: Delilah Books,
    G.P. Putnam's Sons, 1981.

Glass, Lillian, Ph.D. Talk to Win: Six Steps to a
    Successful Vocal Image. Perigree Books, 1987.

Goodwin, Donald W. Anxiety. New York: Oxford
    University Press: 1986.

Hagen, Uta with Frankel, Haskel. _Respect for Acting_.
New York: Macmillan Publishing Co., Inc., 1973.

Harvey, Joan C., Ph.D. and Katz, Cynthia. _If I'm So
Successful, Why Do I Feel Like a Fake: The
Imposter Phenomenon_. New York: St. Martin's
Press, 1985.

Hatterer, Lawrence J., M.D. _The Artist in Society:
Problems and Treatment of the Creative
Personality_. New York: Grove Press, Inc., 1965.

Havas, Kato. _Stage Fright - Its Causes and Cures with
Special Reference to Violin Playing_. London:
Bosworth & Co., Ltd., 1973.

Hawes, William. _The Performer in Mass Media_. New
York: Hastings House, 1978.

Hines, Jerome. _Great Singers on Great Singing_. New
York: Doubleday & Co., 1982.

Hyams, Joe. _Zen in the Martial Arts_. Los Angeles:
J.P. Tarcher, Inc., 1979.

Hyde, Margaret. _Mind Drugs_. New York: Pocket Books,
1969.

Jampolsky, Gerald G., M.D. _Love is Letting Go of Fear_.
Berkeley: Celestial Arts, 1979.

LeShan, Lawrence. _How to Meditate_. New York: Bantam,
1974.

Lipton, Sampson, ed. _Persistent Pain: Modern Methods
of Treatment_. London: Academic Press, 1980.

Maclis, Joseph. _The Career of Magda V._ New York:
Norton & Co., 1985.

Maltz, Maxwell, M.D. _Psychocybenetics_. New York:
Pocket Books, 1960.

Matthews, Andrew. _Being Happy!_ Los Angeles: Price
Stern Sloan, 1988.

McCluggage, Denise. _The Centered Skier_. New York:
Bantam, 1983.

McCullough, Christopher, Ph.D. <u>Always at Ease:</u>
<u>Overcoming Anxiety and Shyness in Every</u>
<u>Situation.</u>Los Angeles: Jeremy P. Tarcher, Inc.,
1991.

McQuade, Walter and Aikman, Ann. <u>Stress: What It Is,</u>
<u>What It Can Do to Your Health, How to Fight Back</u>.
New York: Dutton, 1974.

Moore, Sonia. <u>The Stanislavsky System in Class</u>.
New York: Penguin Books, 1979.

Olivier, Laurence. <u>Confessions of an Actor</u>.
Penguin Books, 1982.

Olshan, Dr. Neal and Wang, Julie. <u>Everything You</u>
<u>Wanted to Know About Phobias But Were Afraid to</u>
<u>Ask</u>. New York and Toronto: Beaufort Books, Inc.,
1981.

Pelletier, Kenneth R. <u>Mind as Healer, Mind as Slayer</u>:
<u>Holistic Approach to Preventing Stress Disorders</u>.
New York: Dell, 1977.

Sheehan, George, M.D. <u>How to Feel Great 24 Hours a</u>
<u>Day</u>. New York: Simon and Schuster, 1983.

Sheehy, Gail. <u>Passages</u>. New York: Bantam Books,
1974.

_____. <u>Pathfinders</u>. New York: Bantam Books, 1982.

Peale, Norman Vincent. <u>Positive Imaging: The Powerful</u>
<u>Way to Change Your Life</u>. New York: Fawcett
Crest, 1982.

_____. <u>The True Joy of Positive Living</u>. New York:
William Morrow & Co., Inc., 1984.

Pease, Victor. <u>Anxiety into Energy</u>. New York:
Hawthorne Dutton, 1981.

Peters, Thomas J. and Waterman, Robert H., Jr.
<u>In Search of Excellence</u>, New York: Harper and
Row, 1982.

Plaskin, Glenn. <u>Horowitz: A Biography</u>. New York:
Wilson Morrow and Company, 1983.

Quick, Thomas L. <u>Power Plays</u> New York: 1985.

Ratliff, Gerald Lee. <u>Coping with Stagefright</u>. New
    York: The Rosen Publishing Group, Inc., 1985.

Ristead, Eloise. <u>A Soprano in Her Head</u>. Utah: Real
    People Press, 1982.

Reubart, Dale. <u>Anxiety and Musical Performance: On
    Playing the Piano from Memory</u>. New York: DaCapo
    Press, 1985.

Rogers, Henry C. <u>Rogers' Rules for Success</u>. Marek:
    St. Martin's Press, 1914.

Rogers, Natalie H. <u>Talk Power: How to Speak without
    Fear - A Systematic Training Program</u>. New York:
    Dodd, Mead and Company, 1982.

<u>Royal Canadian Air Force Exercise Plans for Physical
    Fitness</u>, New York: Simon & Schuster, Inc., 1962.

Sanders, Antoinette and Remsberg, Bonnie. <u>The
    Stress-Proof Child</u>. New York: Holt, Rinehart and
    Winston, 1984.

Sarnoff, Dorothy with Moore, Gaylen. <u>Never Be Nervous
    Again</u>. New York: Crown Publishers, Inc., 1987.

Schuller, Robert H. <u>Tough Times Never Last, But Tough
    People Do</u>. Thomas Nelson Publishers, 1983.

Selye, Hans, M.D. <u>The Stress of Life</u>. McGraw-Hill
    Book Company, 1956.

Selye, Hans, M.D. <u>Stress Without Distress</u>. New York:
    Signet, 1974.

Sher, Barbara with Gottlieb, Annie. <u>Wishcraft: How to
    Get What You Really Want</u>. New York: Ballantine,
    1979.

Silver, Fred. <u>Auditioning for the Musical Theater</u>.
    Newmarket Press, 1985.

Singer, Jerome L. and Switzer, Ellen. <u>Mind Play:
    The Creative Uses of Fantasy</u>. New York: Spectrum
    Books, 1980.

Smith, Manuel J., Ph.D. <u>Kicking the Fear Habit</u> New
    York: Dial Press, 1977.

Smith, Philip. <u>Total Breathing</u>. New York:
    McGraw-Hill Book Company, 1980.

Spiegel, Herbert, M.D. <u>The Inner Source: Exploring</u>
    <u>Hypnosis</u>. New York: Holt Rheinhart & Winston,
    Owl Books, 1984.

Spiegel, Herbert, M.D. and Spiegel, David, M.D. <u>Trance</u>
    <u>and Treatment: Clinical Uses of Hypnosis</u>. New
    York: Basic Books, Inc., 1984.

Stone, Janet and Bachner, Jane. <u>Speaking Up: A Book</u>
    <u>for Every Woman Who Wants to Speak Effectively</u>.
    New York: McGraw-Hill Book Company, 1977.

Suinn, Robert M., Ph.D. <u>Seven Steps to Peak</u>
    <u>Performance</u>: <u>The Mental Training Manual for</u>
    <u>Athletes</u>. Toronto: Hans Huber Publishers, 1986.

Swede, Shirley and Jaffe, Seymour Sheppard, M.D.
    <u>The Panic Attack Recovery Book</u>. New York:
    Penguin Books, New American Library, 1987.

Tec, Leon, M.D. <u>The Fear of Success</u>. Signet, New
    American Library, 1976.

Triplett, Robert. <u>Stagefright: Letting It Work For</u>
    <u>You</u>. Chicago: Nelson-Hall, 1983.

Viscott, David, M.D. <u>The Viscott Method</u>. New York:
    Pocket Books, 1984.

Waitley, Denis. <u>Seeds of Greatness: The Ten Best-Kept</u>
    <u>Secrets of Total Success</u>. Old Tappan, New Jersey:
    Fleming H. Revell Company, 1983.

Weatherspoon, Ricky and Wall, Joan. <u>Anyone Can Sing</u>.
    New York: Doubleday and Co., Inc. 1978.

Wolpe, Jospeh, M.D. <u>Life Without Fear</u>. 1988.

Microfilms

Fanelli, Gerard C. "The effect of need for achievement
    and locus-of-control on performance, level of
    aspiration behaviors." University Microfilms
    International, 1983.

Appel, Sylvia S. "Modifying solo performance anxiety
    in adult pianists." University Microfilms
    International, 1983.

Articles

Alfano, Peter. "McEnroe - A need for respect."
New York Times May 6, 1985.

Anderson, Richard, M.D. "Anxiety attacks: Teaching
patients to conquer fears." Consultant Aug 1983.

Balamori, Marilyn. "Hypnotist Harvey Misel casts a
spell on the White Sox." People Weekly,
Sept, 1983.

Braden, Vic. "How to deal with tournament pressure."
Tennis Magazine.

Brantigan, Charles O., M.D., Brantigan, Thomas A.,
D.M.A., and Joseph, Neil, M.D. "Beta blockade and
musical performance." Lancet, Oct 21, 1978: 896.

_____. The effect of beta blockade and beta
stimulation on stage fright: a controlled study."
Am J Medicine Jan 1982, 72: 88-93.

Breo, Dennis L. "Stress and success: The key is
control." Facets July, 1985: 26-28.

Brody, Jane. "Panic attacks: The terror is
treatable."New York Times Oct 19, 1983.

Burke, Bonnie. "My nights and daze in a sensory
deprivation tank." Cosmopolitan May, 1982.

Carey, Robert M. "Clinical applications of relaxation
training." Hospital Practice, July, 1983.

Clark, Duncan B., Ph.D., M.D. and Agras, W. Stewart,
M.D. "The assessment and treatment of performance
anxiety in musicians." Am J Psychiatry 148:5,
May, 1991: 598.

Coleman, Daniel. "Social anxiety: New focus leads to
insight and therapy." New York Times Dec 18,
1987.

Conway, Michael   "Final examinations." Practitioner
     June, 1971, 206: 795.

Cummings, Sally. "Fear free."   Health November, 1987.

Davis, Joel. "Anxiety Aches." Self Jan, 1985.

Dunning, Jennifer. "The new American actor." New York
     Times Oct 2, 1983.

Dyer, Wayne. "24 ways to have a hassle-free and happy
     holiday season." Family Circle, Jan 3, 1984.

Eliasch, Rosen. "Propranolol in acute anxiety and
     stage fright." British Heart Journal 1967: 29,
     671.

Ferrell, Tom. "Some sad people it seems are unhappy as
     a matter of habit." New York Times Nov 15, 1983.

Finn, Joan A. "Competitive excellence: It's a matter
     of mind and body." The Physician and Sports
     Medicine Feb, 1985.

Fitz, Reginald. "Be smarter, just eat the right
     foods."Esquire Sept 20, 1983.

Flanagan, Patrick. "How to win friends, influence
     people, and create an empire." MD May, 1983.

Frankenhaeuser, M. "Behavioral efficiency as related
     to adrenalin release." Paper presented at the
     'Symposium Stress et Fatigue' Permanent Commission
     and International Association on Occupational
     Health, Paris, Oct, 1968.

Greenspan, Emily. "Conditioning athletes' minds." New
     York Times Magazine Aug 28, 1983.

Hamann, Donald L. "The other side of stage fright."
     MEJ April, 1985: 26-28.

Hanley, Mary Ann. "Creative visualization: Antidote
     to performance anxiety?" The American Music
     Teacher July, 1984: 28-29.

Hannon, Sharron. "Ways to Unwind." Cosmopolitan
     May, 1982.

Hartley, L.R., Ungapen, S., Davie, I., and Spencer, J. "The effect of beta adrenergic blocking drugs on speakers' performance and memory." <u>Brit J Psychiat</u> 1983, 142, pp. 512-517.

Henahan, Donal. "But do we want to banish stage fright."<u>New York Times</u>, August 8, 1982: 15.

Heymont, George. "Ned Rorem lays it on the line." <u>Ovation</u> Oct, 1983: 23-26.

Holland, Bernard. "It takes more than talent to build a musical career." <u>New York Times</u>, Feb 19, 1984.

Holland, Bernard. "Making music can be harmful to one's health." <u>New York Times</u> May 6, 1985.

Horvitz, Deborah J., "Understanding phobias." <u>HealthWays</u> Vol. II, No.3, Sept, 1989, p. 10.

Hunt, Morton. "Self hypnosis works." <u>Reader's Digest</u> Apr, 1984.

Jacobsen, Robert. "Once more with feeling: Soprano Graziella Sciotti." <u>Opera News</u>, Dec 22, 1984.

James, I.M., Griffith, D.N.W., Pearson, R.M., and Newbury, Patricia. "Effect of oxyprenolol on stage-fright in musicians." <u>Lancet</u> Nov 5, 1977: 952-954.

Jerome, John. "The training effect." <u>Esquire</u> June, 1980.

Kaercher, Dan. "The uses and abuses of mood altering drugs." <u>Better Homes and Gardens</u> May, 1983.

_____. "Hypnosis: How modern medicine is using an ancient art." <u>Better Homes and Gardens</u> Oct 1983: 24-32.

Keller, Barbara. "Stage fright and how to conquer it."

<u>Keynote</u> July 1983: 22-25.

Kelly, Evelyn B., Ph.D. "Imagery as management tool." <u>Sky</u>, Jan, 1990. p. 102.

Klass, Roseanne. "Pavarotti: As passionate about teaching as singing." <u>New York Times</u> Jan 20, 1980.

Klemesrud, Judy. "Speech classes help women at the podium." New York Times Aug 11, 1983.

Kosslyn, Stephen M., "Stalking the mental image." Psychology Today May 1985: 23-28.

Larkin, Marilynn. "Your emotions/your voice." Vogue May, 1984.

Lawrence, Linda. "Stages of faith: A conversation with James Fowler." Psychology Today Nov, 1983.

Lehrer, Paul M. "A Review of the Approaches to the management of tension and stage fright in music performance." Journal of Research In Musical Education Vol. 35, No. 3, 1987, pp. 143-152.

Lewis, Robert. "She inspired Stanislavsky." New York Times Book Review Sept 30, 1984.

Liversidge, Anthony. "The confidence pill." New York Magazine, Jan 28, 1980, pp. 34-36.

Margold, Jane A. "Hypnosis: What it can do for you." Avenue Oct 1984.

Mayers, Hillary and Babits, Linda. "A balanced approach: The Alexander technique." MEJ Nov 1987.

Michalski, Stanley F., Jr. "The best you can be: Criteria for self-evaluation." Music Educators' Journal Sept, 1983.

Michener, Charles. "Acting can be fun." Newsweek July 26, 1982.

Mitgang, Herbert. "When actors review the audience." New York Times Apr 21, 1983.

Moleskey, Grace. "Boost your brain power." Prevention Jan, 1985.

Normand, Patricia, M.D. "Controlling performance anxiety." Drug Therapy May 1985: 11-24.

Perin, Charles T., Ph.D. "The use of substitute response signals in anxiety situations." Am J Clinical Hypnosis Jan 1968: 207.

Peterson, Norma. "Stress." Working Woman Aug 1983.

Pines, Maya. "What you eat can affect your brain."
    Reader's Digest Sept 1983.

Pines, Maya. "When your body is afraid." American
    Health June 1984: 72.

Rickels, J. "Panic disorder may respond to new
    anti-depressants." JAMA Dec 17, 1982, 248:73.

Robbie, Vic. "Amazing new pill overcomes fear, anxiety
    and even shyness." National Enquirer, Feb 4,
    1980.

Rockwell, John. "Hildegard Behrens: New Wagnerian
    queen has emerged at the Met." New York Times,
    Nov 10, 1983.

Rorem, Ned. "Drugs and performers." Ovation
    Oct 1983.

Rose, Phyllis. "Unlike a failure, a success can raise
    unsettling issues." New York Times Apr 19, 1984.

Sarnoff, Alvin P. and Scherer, Ron. "How drugs
    threaten to ruin pro sports." U.S. News and World
    Report Sept 12, 1983.

Seliger, Susan. "Stress can be good for you." New York
    Magazine Aug 2, 1982.

Solway, Diane. "Dancing with the audience." New York
    Times Dec 18, 1983.

Spiegel, David, M.D. "Hypnosis in clinical practice."
    Drug Therapy May, 1983: 173.

Swartz, Conrad. "Propranolol abuse of performer's
    maturation." Lancet Nov 18, 1978: 1105.

Tanne, Janice Hopkins and Rapp, Ellen. "Fearing the
    worst: Tips on conquering paralyzing anxiety."
    New York Feb 9, 1987.

Waitley, Denis. "What makes a winner: The secrets of
    success may be simpler than you thought."
    Reader's Digest, Nov, 1983.

Whiting, Joshua C. "Hypnosis and music = creativity:
    A holistic approach." Hypnosis Quarterly,
    Vol. XXV, No. 4, 1982.

"Actors all alone in the spotlight." <u>New York Times</u>
     Oct 5, 1984.

"Athletes are put in the right frame of mind." <u>New
     York Times</u> Sept 8, 1981.

"Beta blockers seen to inhibit type A behavior and
     risks." <u>Cardiology Times</u>, Nov 1983.

"Beta block that stage fright."   <u>Emergency Medicine</u>
     May 15, 1982: 167.

"Bravissimo, Domingo." <u>Newsweek</u> Mar 18, 1983.

"Doctors hit on a confidence pill that can turn you
     into a winner." <u>The Star</u> Feb 4, 1980.

"Fast lane living: Some people are perhaps addicted to
     stress." <u>Cardiovascular News</u> Sept, 1983.

"The fight to conquer fear." <u>Newsweek</u> Apr 23, 1984:
     66.

"Hypnosis still no panacea but the pendulum is swinging
     again." <u>Medical News</u>, Feb 6, 1978.

"Jessye Norman." <u>New York Times</u> Sept 18, 1983.

"Kitty Carlisle Hart ready to return to Broadway."
     <u>New York Times</u> June 14, 1983.

"Leon Fleisher's long journey back to the keyboard."
     <u>New York Times Magazine</u> Sept 12, 1982.

"Looking great, feeling great." <u>Ladies Home Journal</u>
     Nov 1983.

"Musicians whose hands are out of tune get a workup by
     Massachusetts General physicians." <u>Medical World
     News</u> July 19, 1982.

"Olympian drug scandal." <u>Newsweek</u> Sept 5, 1983.

"Panic attacks." <u>Acute Care Medicine</u> May 1984.

"Relax: Relaxation therapy in hypertension." <u>Hospital
     Practice</u> May, 1983.

186

"A review of the approaches to the management of
    tension and stage fright in music performance."
    <u>Journal of Research</u> <u>in Music Education</u> Vol. 3,
    No. 3, 1987, pp. 143-152.

"Science and music." <u>Science Digest</u>, June 1982.

"Shirley MacLaine - A Broadway review." <u>New York Times</u>
    Apr 20, 1984.

"A simple way to feel better." <u>Prevention</u> Rodale
    Press, 1984.

"Stress: Can we cope?." <u>Time</u> June 6, 1983, p. 48.

"Taking drugs on the job." <u>Newsweek</u> Aug 22, 1983.

"Yoga breathing: The key to energy, vitality,
    tranquility." <u>Ladies Home Journal</u> Nov 1983: 66.

"Yoga - the gentle body builder." <u>Vogue</u> Oct 1983.